ALL-TIME BAKING FAVORITES

Editor: JoAnne Alter
Art Director: Marsha J. Camera
Associate Editor: Lyle Lawson
Art Associate: Walter C. Schwartz
Production Manager: Norman Ellers

Cover photograph by Bill McGinn
How-to diagrams by Adolph Brotman
Illustrations by Oni

All recipes tested in Family Circle's Test Kitchens

Created by Family Circle Magazine and published 1978 by Arno Press Inc., a subsidiary of The New York Times Company. Copyright © 1974 by The Family Circle, Inc. All rights reserved. Protected under Berne and other international copyright conventions. Title and Trademark FAMILY CIRCLE registered U.S. Patent and Trademark Office, Canada, Great Britain, Australia, New Zealand, Japan and other countries. Marca Registrada. This volume may not be reproduced in whole or in part in any form without written permission from the publisher. Printed in U.S.A. Library of Congress Catalog Card Number 78-56968. ISBN 0-405-11406-0.

A New York Times Company Publication

CONTENTS

1 Baking Facts 5

2 Yeast Breads & Rolls 17

3 Quick Breads 47

4 Cakes & Frostings 55

5 Cookies 81

6 Pies & Tarts 101

7 Specialties 119

8 Terrific Time-Savers 137

   Index 142

Here are just a few of our All-Time Baking Favorites. From top, down: Burnt Sugar Cake; Grandmother's White Bread and Anadama Cheese Bread; Chocolate Chip Cookies, Oatmeal Crunchies, and Country Cherry Pie. Recipes for all are listed in the Index.

1

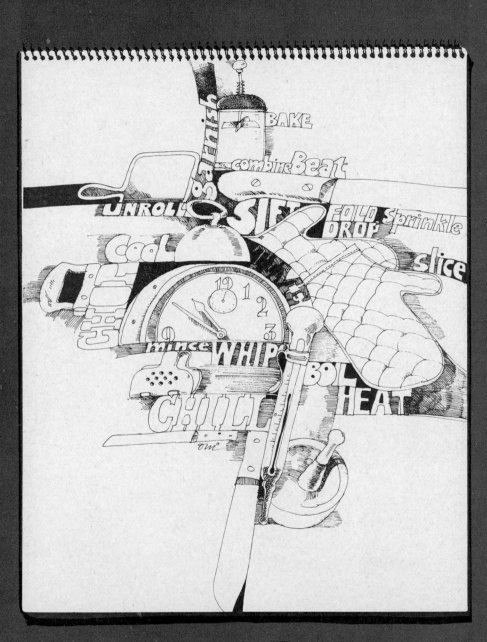

BAKING FACTS

Our first chapter is packed with baking basics! In it, you'll find helpful hints and how-to's—everything you need to know to bake, store, freeze and serve the best breads, rolls and baked desserts you ever made. You're sure to find it invaluable!

KINDS OF PANS

If you don't already have the following on hand, they're well worth the investment. (All new pans are stamped on the bottom, to indicate size):

Round pans—two 8-inch; two 9-inch
Square pans—two 8-inch; two 9-inch
Oblong pans—one 13x9x2-inch
Pie plates—two 9-inch
Loaf pans—two 9x5x3-inch
Jelly roll pan—one 15½ x10½ x1-inch
Bundt tube pan—one 9-inch cast aluminum, with nonstick coating
Spring-form pan—one 9-inch with removable bottom
Angel cake tube pan—one 10-inch with removable bottom
Muffin pans—two, 12 muffins each, 2½-in. diameter
Oven-proof custard cups (for popovers)—6 to 8
Cooky sheets—two; the biggest ones that will fit your oven, allowing at least one inch all around for proper circulation

The following aren't essential, but they're nice to have:

Ring mold—one 9¼ x2¾ -inch
Kugelhupf pan—one 10x4-inch
Fluted quiche pan—one 9-in. with removable bottom
Individual tart pans—6 to 8, fluted or plain
Small gem pan(s)—one or two, 12 small muffins each, 1¼ -inch diameter
Heavy iron popover pan—one for 6 popovers
Madeleine pan—one for 12 cookies

Note: Round pans, square pans, small pie plates (7- to 8-inch), small loaf pans (8-inch) and small tart pans (3-inch) are generally available in reusable aluminum foil. You can buy them in department, hardware and variety stores.

ALTERNATE PAN CHART*

If your recipe calls for:	You may use:
Two 8x1½-inch round pans	18 to 24 (2½-inch) cupcake pan cups
Three 8x1½-inch round pans	Two 9x9x2-inch square pans; or one 13x9x2-inch oblong pan
Two 9x1½-inch round pans	Two 8x8x2-inch square pans; or one 13x9x2-inch oblong pan
One 9x5x3-inch loaf pan	One 9x9x2-inch square pan
Two 9x5x3-inch loaf pans	One 10x4-inch tube pan
One 8x4x3-inch loaf pan	One 8x8x2-inch square pan
One 9x3½-inch angel cake pan	One 10x3¾-inch bundt pan; or one 9x3½-inch fancy tube pan

*Note: This chart applies to butter cakes only. Chiffon, pound, sponge and angel food cakes are best baked in the pans specifically called for in recipes.

From top to bottom:
*Round Pan,
Square Pan,
Pie Plate,
Loaf Pan,
Jelly Roll Pan,
Spring-form.*

From top to bottom: Bundt Pan, Angel Cake Tube Pan, Muffin Pan, Ring Mold, Kugelhupf.

SPECIAL TIPS: Many pans are now available in either metal or glass. You can use either. But remember, ovenproof glass conducts heat more than metal does; so if you do use glass pans, always lower the oven temperature by *25 degrees*.

• Also, glass pans hold slightly less in volume than do metal pans. The difference isn't critical in most recipes, but you can expect your bread or cake to be slightly higher if you bake it in a glass pan.

OTHER EQUIPMENT YOU'LL WANT TO HAVE

Measuring and Mixing:
Flour sifter
Dry measuring cups—nested in sets from ¼ cup to 1 cup
Measuring spoons, also in sets, from ¼ teaspoon to 1 tablespoon
Liquid measuring cup—either one-, two- or four-cup size
Mixing bowls (small, medium, large)
Wooden spoons—set of three or four
Electric mixer—either standard or portable
Wire whisk—for combining and folding ingredients, keeping cooking mixtures smooth, and beating eggs
Pastry blender—for cutting shortening into flour, when making pastry. You can also use 2 knives, cutting in opposite directions next to each other.
Rubber scrapers—standard size and thin
18-inch ruler—for measuring pans and rolled-out dough
Small funnel

Rolling and Shaping:
Pastry board—for rolling and working with dough. Actually, any clean, dry, flat surface dusted with flour is fine.
Rolling pin
2-inch biscuit cutter (Try using an empty orange juice can.)
Kitchen scissors—for trimming pie crusts, cutting dried fruits, etc.
Cooky gun—metal tube with a variety of cut-out discs, to form cookies of different shapes
Cooky cutters—assorted shapes (For directions on how to trace and make your own cooky cutters, see pages 84 and 85.)

Cooking and Baking:
2- or 3-quart heavy saucepan
Double boiler
Kitchen timer—if your oven doesn't have one

Lifting and Cooling:
Wide spatula or pancake turner
Three wire racks for cooling cakes and cookies (You can also use your oven racks for cooling baked goods.)

Frosting and Decorating:
Straight-edged spatula—a must for frosting; also useful for leveling dry ingredients, lifting cookies, loosening cakes

Canvas pastry bag—for shaping eclairs, cream puffs, meringue layers; for decorating and garnishing cakes. (You can select tips to fit your pastry bag.) Also, for quick shaping of drop cookies.

Cake decorating set (metal tube plus assorted tips)—for decorating cakes and cookies. (For directions on how to make a disposable wax paper decorating bag to use with your own decorating tips, see page 13.)

ABOUT INGREDIENTS IN THIS BOOK

Butter and margarine: Either is fine. *Recipes in this book were tested with both.* Use only stick form, not whipped or diet.

Eggs: *All recipes were tested using large eggs.*

Flour: Important—All white flour (all-purpose and cake) must be sifted before measuring. Rye and whole wheat flour needn't be.
• All-purpose flour—milled from both hard and soft wheat; for all baking other than cakes.
• Cake flour—milled from soft wheat; for all cakes.
• Rye flour—used with other flours in making breads, e.g., with all-purpose flour for rye bread.
• Whole wheat flour—milled from hard wheat, with bits of whole grain remaining. Used with all-purpose flour to make whole wheat bread.

Leavening agents:
• Baking powder—principal leavening agent for quick breads. *All recipes in this book use double-action baking powder.*
• Baking soda—also called bicarbonate of soda; helps neutralize acids, such as brown sugar. Since baking soda loses its potency with age, it's a good idea to buy it in small cans.
• Cream of tartar—helps stabilize foams, such as meringues.
• Yeast—either active dry yeast (in granular form) or compressed yeast (in cake form) is fine. *Note:* You may want to use active dry yeast, however, since it lasts longer than compressed yeast and needs no refrigeration. In either case, always use yeast before its expiration date, to guarantee proper results.

Milk products:
• Buttermilk—whole, skim or nonfat milk that has been soured.
• Evaporated milk—whole milk from which 60% of the water has been removed.
• Heavy cream—contains between 36% and 40% butterfat.
• Light cream—contains between 18% and 30% butterfat.
• Milk (whole)—*Unless otherwise specified, used in all recipes calling for milk.*
• Sour cream—light cream that has been soured; contains between 18% and 20% butterfat.
• Sweetened condensed milk—whole milk with half the water removed and sugar added.

Shortening: Soft vegetable shortening comes in solid form; it's available in one-, two- and three-pound cans. Used in pastry, cookies and some cakes. *Unless otherwise specified, always grease pans with solid shortening.*

Sugars and syrups:
• Brown sugar (both light and dark)—the darker the color, the more the flavor of molasses. When measuring, be sure to pack firmly!
• Corn syrup (both light and dark)—for pies, some frostings.
• Granulated sugar—the kind in your sugar bowl. *Unless otherwise specified, used in all recipes calling for sugar.*
• Honey—used mainly in cookies and coffee cakes.
• Molasses—processed from sugar cane; used primarily in cookies and spice cakes.
• 10X (confectioners' or powdered) sugar—crushed sugar blended with cornstarch. Sometimes used instead of frosting; used in all butter cream frostings. (If your 10X sugar has gotten lumpy, sift before using.)

Thickening agents:
• Cornstarch—used to thicken pie and cake fillings; also used in dessert sauces.
• Tapioca—used to thicken fruit pies.

Vegetable oil: Any type (corn, peanut, safflower, etc.) is fine. Usually used in chiffon cakes and quick breads. Use only where specified.

GLOSSARY

Bake	To cook by means of dry heat, usually in an oven
Batter	A mixture of flour and liquid plus other ingredients; thin enough to drop or pour
Beat	To make a mixture smooth or to introduce air by using a vigorous, steady over-and-over motion
Blend	To gently, but thoroughly, mix two or more ingredients together
Boil	To cook a liquid or in a liquid in which bubbles break on surface (212° F. at sea level)
Caramelize	To heat sugar slowly until it becomes brown in color and caramel in flavor
Chop	To cut food into fine pieces with knife or mechanical chopper
Cream	To blend two or more foods, usually butter or margarine and sugar, until smooth and fluffy
Cut	To combine shortening or liquid with dry ingredients using pastry blender or two knives
Dissolve	To make a solution from a dry and a liquid ingredient
Dough	A mixture of flour and liquid plus other ingredients; stiff enough to knead or roll
Fold	To combine ingredients using an up-over-and-down motion

SPECIAL LOW-CALORIE TIPS

You can enjoy baked breads, cakes, cookies and pies, even if you're watching your weight! You'll find a number of sensational Low Calorie recipes in this book. In addition, the following tips, from *Family Circle's* "Creative Low Calorie Cooking" series, by Barbara Gibbons, are some of the best ways to trim calories from almost any recipe:

- When recipes call for sour cream, try yogurt or buttermilk as a substitute, and eliminate four-fifths of the calories.

- Soy flour, which is slightly lower in calories and carbohydrates, but much richer in proteins than all-purpose flour, can be used to replace up to one-third of the flour in any recipe. You can find it in health food stores and some supermarkets.

- Use evaporated skim milk instead of heavy cream and cut calories by three-fourths.

- Any cake will be bigger and higher (which means more slices at fewer calories) if you separate the eggs and whip the whites stiff before adding them to the batter. Try it—even if the recipe doesn't call for this step.

- You can, in most cases, get chocolate flavor without chocolate calories by using cocoa in place of un-sweetened (baking) chocolate. Instead of one ounce of solid chocolate (143 calories), use 3 table-spoons unsweetened cocoa (60 calories). Better yet, instead of one tablespoon cocoa, use one tea-spoon chocolate extract (only 7 calories!)

- If, in addition to calories, you must watch your cholesterol level, substitute two egg whites, stiffly beaten and folded into cake batter, for each whole egg called for in the recipe.

- Pie crusts are the most calorific part of most pies. Chill the dough very well and roll crusts extra-thin, and you'll have fewer calories per portion.

- Sugar substitutes can really help to rescue a pie from the forbidden list. If you can't stand a pie totally made from sugar substitutes, use a mixture of half sugar, half substitute. This will drastically alter the calorie count without substantially chang-ing the taste.

- A well-fruited pie needs less thickener than does a skimpy one. Use cornstarch instead of flour to thicken any fruit pie. Both have 29 calories per tablespoon, but with cornstarch, you need only half as much!

- Spices add everything to a pie—except calories; so spice up any pie to suit your taste. A touch of vanilla can heighten the impression of sweetness, while such extracts as orange, lemon, brandy or rum are terrific flavor enhancers.

9

Knead	To work dough with the hands, using a pressing and folding motion until dough is smooth and elastic
Sift	To put dry ingredients through a sieve
Simmer	To cook a liquid or in a liquid at a temperature just below boiling. Bubbles form slowly and break just below the surface
Stir	To mix with a spoon, using circular motion
Whip	To beat rapidly to incorporate air and increase volume

HOW TO MEASURE INGREDIENTS

When measuring any ingredient, the key word to remember is "level".

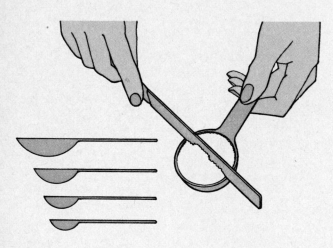

Make sure all dry ingredients measured in spoons or cups are leveled off at the top, with the edge of a knife, or with a straight-edged spatula.

Important: All white flour must be measured *after it has been sifted*. Spoon sifted flour lightly into measuring cup and level off. Do not tap the cup or in any way pack the flour down.

Brown sugar and solid shortening *should* be packed firmly in a measuring spoon or cup, then leveled off.

Measure liquids in a glass measuring cup, placed on a table or counter. Fill to the appropriate line, checking measurement at eye level.

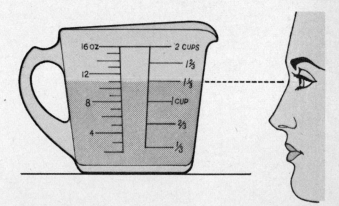

IMPORTANT MEASURES

1½ teaspoons	= ½ tablespoon
3 teaspoons	= 1 tablespoon
2 tablespoons	= 1 ounce
4 tablespoons	= ¼ cup
5 tablespoons plus 1 teaspoon	= ⅓ cup
8 tablespoons	= ½ cup
10 tablespoons plus 2 teaspoons	= ⅔ cup
12 tablespoons	= ¾ cup
16 tablespoons	= 1 cup (8 ounces)
2 cups	= 1 pint
2 pints	= 1 quart
4 quarts	= 1 gallon

EASY EQUIVALENTS

FOOD	EQUIVALENT
Eggs:	
Whole eggs, 1 cup	About 6 large
Egg yolks, 1 cup	11 to 12
Egg whites, 1 cup	7 to 8
Fruit:	
Apples, 1 pound	3 medium (3 cups sliced)
Lemon, 1 medium	2 teaspoons grated rind plus 2 tablespoons juice
Orange, 1 medium	4 teaspoons grated rind plus ⅓ cup orange juice
Strawberries, 1 quart	3½ cups hulled
Milk products:	
Butter or margarine	
1 pound	4 sticks or 2 cups
4 tablespoons	½ stick or ¼ cup
Heavy cream, 1 cup	2 cups, whipped
Ice cream, ½ gallon	4 pints
Milk, evaporated	
Small can (5⅓ ounces)	⅔ cup
Tall can (13 ounces)	1⅔ cups
Milk, sweetened condensed	
(14 ounces)	1⅔ cups
Nuts:	
Almonds, shelled, 1 pound	3½ cups
Peanuts, shelled, 1 pound	3 cups
Pecans, shelled, 1 pound	4 cups
Walnuts, shelled, 1 pound	4 cups
Starches:	
Flour, all-purpose, 1 pound	4 cups, sifted
Flour, cake, 1 pound	4½ cups plus 2 tablespoons, sifted
Graham crackers, 11 squares	1 cup crumbs
Sugars:	
Brown, 1 pound	2¼ cups, packed
Granulated, 1 pound	2 cups
10X (confectioners'), 1 pound	About 4 cups

SIMPLE SUBSTITUTIONS

INSTEAD OF	USE
Baking powder, 1 teaspoon	¼ teaspoon baking soda plus ⅝ teaspoon cream of tartar
Buttermilk, 1 cup	1 tablespoon lemon juice or vinegar plus sweet milk to equal 1 cup. (Let mixture stand for about 5 minutes.)
Chocolate, unsweetened 1 square, (1 ounce)	3 tablespoons cocoa plus 1 tablespoon fat.
Cornstarch, 1½ teaspoons	1 tablespoon flour
Corn syrup, 1 cup	1 cup sugar plus ¼ cup liquid
Egg, 1 whole	2 egg yolks
Honey, 1 cup	1¼ cups sugar plus ¼ cup liquid
Milk, skim, 1 cup	⅓ cup instant nonfat dry milk plus 1 cup minus 1 tablespoon water.
Milk, whole, 1 cup	½ cup evaporated milk plus ½ cup water.
Tapioca, 2 teaspoons	1 tablespoon flour

HIGH ALTITUDE TIPS

Unless you live at least 3,000 feet above sea level, you probably won't have to make any adjustments. Above that, you may wish to make the following changes:

Altitude	*3,000 to 4,000 feet*	*4,000 to 6,000 feet*	*6,000 to 7,500 feet*
Reduce Baking Powder For each teaspoon, decrease	⅛ tsp.	⅛ to ¼ tsp.	¼ tsp.
Reduce Sugar For each cup, decrease	1 Tbs.	1 to 2 Tbs.	3 to 4 Tbs.
Increase Liquid For each cup, add	1 to 2 Tbs.	2 to 4 Tbs.	3 to 4 Tbs.
Baking Temperature	Increase 25°	Increase 25°	Increase 25°

• For particularly rich butter or shortening cakes, try reducing the shortening by 1 or 2 tablespoons.

• If you live at an extremely high altitude, you may wish to increase the amount of egg in angel food, chiffon or sponge cakes.

• Only by experimenting will you find the right modifications for your needs. Try the smaller adjustments on any recipe the first time you make it; then, next time, if necessary, make the larger adjustment.

The chart below shows how many servings you can get from each cake or coffee cake you bake. The diagrams below demonstrate the easiest ways to cut the number of slices you want.

SPECIAL TIP: How many servings can you expect to get from a cake? Here's an idea:

9x5x3-inch loaf cake 8
8-inch square ....8 or 9
9-inch square 9
8-inch double layer ....10—12
9-inch double layer ....12—16
13x9x2-inch ....12—16
10-inch bundt or tube cake ....10—12
10-inch jelly roll 10

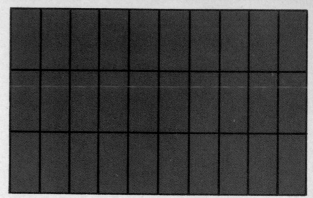

13x9x2-inch single-layer cake
30 servings

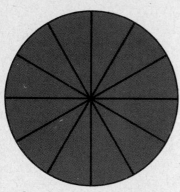

8- or 9-inch double-layer cake
12 servings

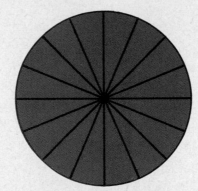

9-inch double-layer cake
16 servings (Good way to cut tortes.)

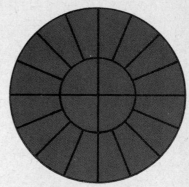

9-inch double-layer cake
20 servings (Good for very rich cakes.)

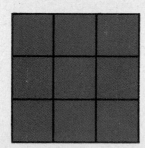

8- or 9-inch single-layer cake
9 servings

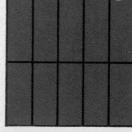

8- or 9-inch single-layer cake
10 servings

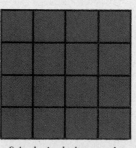

9-inch single-layer cake
16 servings (Good for cakes with
sweet, broiled toppings.)

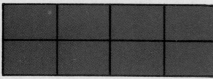

9x5x3-inch loaf
8 servings. (Good for coffee cakes.)

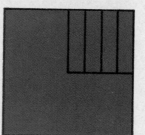

8- or 9-inch double-layer cake
16 servings (Note: Slice square double-layer
cake one quarter at a time, to keep
cake from collapsing.

9x5x3-inch loaf
8 servings (Note: To make 16 wedge-shaped slices,
for topping with ice cream, for example, cut each
of the eight slices in half, diagonally.)

Nutritious whole-grain breads:
Good tasting and good for you, too.
From top, down: High-protein Whole Wheat
Bread, Swedish Limpa, and our glazed,
round Swedish Limpa variation.
Recipes in Chapter 2.

Hot bread, fresh from the oven; what better way to say "Welcome"! Recipe for our inviting Anadama Cheese Bread in this chapter.

2

YEAST BREADS & ROLLS

Experience the sheer joy and satisfaction of baking wholesome and delicious yeast breads. Delight your family with savory, aromatic breads and rolls; warm, sweet coffee cakes and fragrant Danish. They're easy, and economical, too! And they're all in this chapter.

Breads from around the world, to add international flair to any meal. Top left: Irish Soda Bread (recipe, Chapter 3). Other breads shown: braided Challah, dark Scandinavian Rye Bread, saucer-shaped Armenian Breads and long Crusty French loaves. Recipes in this chapter.

as much flour as needed to keep dough from sticking.
4. Place in a greased, large bowl; turn to coat all over with shortening; cover with a clean towel. Let rise in a warm place, away from drafts, 1 hour, or until double in bulk.
5. Punch dough down; turn out onto lightly floured surface; invert bowl over dough; let rest 20 minutes.
6. Grease 2 cooky sheets; sprinkle with cornmeal.
7. Divide dough in half and knead each half a few times. Roll each half to a 15x10-inch rectangle. Roll up tightly from long side, jelly roll fashion; pinch long seams tightly to seal. Roll loaves gently back and forth with hands to taper ends. Place loaves diagonally on prepared cooky sheets.
8. Let rise again in a warm place, away from drafts, 45 minutes, or until double in bulk.
9. Make slits 2 inches apart on top of breads with a very sharp knife or razor blade. Beat egg white and cold water together in a small cup. Brush loaves.
10. Bake in a hot oven (400°) 40 minutes or until golden in color and loaves sound hollow when tapped. Remove from cooky sheets to wire racks; cool completely.

Sourdough Starter: Makes 4 cups.
  2 cups milk
  2 cups sifted all-purpose flour

Pour milk into a glass or ceramic bowl and cover bowl with cheesecloth. Let stand in the outdoors for 1 day. Stir in flour and re-cover bowl with cheesecloth. Place outside for 2 days. Place bowl in a sunny spot indoors and allow to stand until mixture bubbles and starts to sour, about 2 days. Spoon into a quart jar with a screw cap and store in refrigerator at least 1 day before using. (If top of starter should start to dry out at any time during this process, stir in a little lukewarm water.) When you remove 1½ cups of sourdough starter, simply combine ¾ cup milk and ¾ cup flour and stir into jar. Cover jar with cheesecloth and place in sunny spot for 1 day. Remove cheesecloth; cover jar and return to refrigerator.

TAOS BREAD

This Pueblo Indian bread is shaped in the form of the sun—to honor the Sun God.

Bake at 350° for 50 minutes.
Makes 3 loaves.

  1½ cups water
  3 tablespoons butter or margarine
  1 tablespoon sugar
  3 teaspoons salt
  2 envelopes active dry yeast
  ½ cup very warm water
  6½ cups sifted all-purpose flour

1. Combine water, butter or margarine, sugar and salt in a small saucepan. Heat slowly until butter or margarine melts; cool to lukewarm.
2. Sprinkle yeast into very warm water in a large bowl. ("Very warm water" should feel comfortably warm when dropped on wrist.) Stir until yeast dissolves; then stir in butter mixture.
3. Beat in 4 cups of flour until smooth. Beat in enough remaining flour to make a soft dough.
4. Turn out onto a lightly floured surface; knead until smooth and elastic, about 5 minutes, using only as much flour as needed to keep dough from sticking.
5. Place in a greased large bowl; turn to coat all over with shortening; cover with a clean towel. Let rise in a warm place, away from drafts, 1½ hours, or until double in bulk.
6. Punch dough down; turn out onto lightly floured surface; knead a few times; divide dough into 3 equal pieces. Shape each piece into a ball. Cover with a towel, let rest 10 minutes.
7. On the floured surface, roll each ball into a 9-inch circle. Fold each circle almost in half. Top circular edge should be about 1 inch from bottom circular edge. Place on greased cooky sheet. With kitchen scissors, make about 6 gashes in the dough, cutting from the circular edge about ⅔ the way inward to the folded edge. Spread the fingers of dough apart so they will not touch each other while baking. Do the same with the remaining 2 balls of dough. Let rise again in warm place, away from drafts, 1 hour, or until double in bulk.
8. Bake in moderate oven (350°) 50 minutes, or until breads are golden, and sound hollow when tapped. Remove from cooky sheet to wire racks; cool completely.

ARMENIAN BREAD

It looks like a flying saucer and makes a wonderful conversation piece, besides tasting so very good.

Bake at 350° for 30 minutes.
Makes 3 loaves.

  2 envelopes active dry yeast
  2¼ cups very warm water
  ¾ cup nonfat dry milk
  3 tablespoons sugar
  2 teaspoons salt
  3 tablespoons olive or vegetable oil
  6½ cups sifted all-purpose flour
  ¼ cup sesame seeds
  1 egg, beaten

1. Sprinkle yeast into very warm water in a large bowl. ("Very warm water" should feel comfortably warm when dropped on wrist.) Stir until yeast dissolves; then stir in dry milk, sugar, salt and oil.

*Crunchy Butterscotch-Nut Buns, swirled Sugar Buns
and delicate Crumb Cake—all made from the same
basic Sweet Yeast Dough. Recipes in this chapter.*

comfortably warm when dropped on wrist.) Stir until dissolved. Add lukewarm milk mixture and eggs. Blend in flour, 1 cup at a time. Beat until smooth. Stir in currants. Turn into greased 6-cup baking dish.

3. Cover; let rise 45 minutes, or until double in bulk.

4. Bake in a moderate oven (350°) 40 minutes, or until loaf is golden brown and sounds hollow when tapped.

5. Cool a few minutes on wire rack; remove bread from baking dish. Blend 10X sugar and orange juice in a cup. While bread is still warm, drizzle with glaze.

PARMESAN GARLIC BREAD

Get a head start on your next Italian gala by baking this Parmesan Garlic Bread today and freezing it for later. (Don't freeze it all, though—there's enough for you to enjoy some right now!)

Bake at 400° for 40 minutes for large loaves; 30 to 35 minutes for medium-size and small loaves.
Makes 2 large loaves or 8 medium-size loaves or 14 small loaves.

```
  2 cups milk
  2 tablespoons sugar
  2 teaspoons salt
  2 envelopes active dry yeast
  2 cups very warm water
 10 cups sifted all-purpose flour
  1 cup grated Parmesan cheese
  2 tablespoons butter or margarine, melted
  1 clove garlic, crushed
    Grated Parmesan cheese
```

1. Heat milk with sugar and salt in small saucepan just to lukewarm.

2. Sprinkle yeast into very warm water in a large bowl. ("Very warm water" should feel comfortably warm when dropped on wrist.) Stir until yeast dissolves, then stir in cooled milk mixture.

3. Beat in 5 cups flour and 1 cup cheese until completely blended. Beat in remaining flour gradually to make a soft dough.

4. Turn out onto lightly floured surface; knead until smooth and elastic, adding only enough flour to keep dough from sticking.

5. Place in greased large bowl; turn to coat all over with shortening; cover with a clean towel. Let rise in warm place, away from drafts, 1 hour, or until double in bulk. Stir garlic into butter. Brush pans or casseroles with garlic butter.

6. Punch dough down; knead 1 minute on lightly floured surface, then shape this way: For large loaves, divide dough in half, divide each half in 7 even pieces, shape into rolls; place 6 rolls around edge of prepared pan and 1 in center. For medium-size loaves: Divide dough into 16 even pieces; shape into rolls, place 2 rolls in each of 8 prepared ten-ounce casseroles or custard cups. For miniature loaves: Divide dough into 14 pieces; shape into loaves; place in prepared toy-size loaf pans; cover. Let rise again in warm place, away from drafts, 45 minutes, or until double in bulk. Brush tops with water; sprinkle lightly with extra Parmesan cheese.

7. Bake in very hot oven (400°) 40 minutes for large loaves, 30 to 35 minutes for small and medium loaves, or until breads sound hollow when tapped. Remove from pans to wire racks; cool completely.

SWEDISH LIMPA

This orange-scented whole rye and wheat bread has been a Scandinavian favorite for many generations.

Bake at 375° for 45 minutes.
Makes 2 loaves.

```
  2 envelopes active dry yeast
 2½ cups very warm water
  ¼ cup firmly packed brown sugar
  ⅓ cup molasses
  3 tablespoons vegetable shortening
  1 tablespoon salt
  2 tablespoons grated orange rind
  1 teaspoon anise seeds, crushed with hammer
  1 cup cracked wheat
 3½ cups whole rye flour
 3¾ to 4 cups sifted unbleached all-purpose flour
```

1. Sprinkle yeast into ½ cup of the warm water; stir in 1 teaspoon of the brown sugar. ("Very warm water" should feel comfortably warm when dropped on wrist.) Stir until yeast dissolves. Let stand, undisturbed, to proof until bubbly and double in volume, about 10 minutes.

2. Combine remaining water and sugar with molasses, shortening and salt in a small saucepan. Heat until shortening melts; cool to lukewarm.

3. Combine yeast mixture and molasses mixture in large bowl. Add orange rind, anise seeds, cracked wheat and rye flour. Beat with electric mixer at medium speed for 3 minutes. Gradually stir in enough all-purpose flour to make a soft dough.

4. Turn out onto lightly floured surface; knead until smooth and elastic, using remaining all-purpose flour to keep dough from sticking; add more flour, if needed.

5. Place in buttered large bowl; turn to bring greased side up; cover with a towel or plastic wrap. Let rise in a warm place, away from drafts, 1½ hours, or until double in bulk.

6. Punch dough down; turn out onto lightly floured surface; invert bowl over dough; allow to rest 10 minutes. Divide dough in half and knead each half

Fantans: Makes 12 rolls.

¼ recipe Favorite Yeast Rolls
2 tablespoons butter or margarine, melted

Roll out dough to an 18x9-inch rectangle on a lightly floured surface. Cut into twelve 1½-inch wide strips. Brush with melted butter. Stack 6 strips on top of each other to make two stacks. Cut each stack into six 1½-inch wide pieces. Place each piece of the cut stack, cut-side down, into a greased muffin-pan cup.

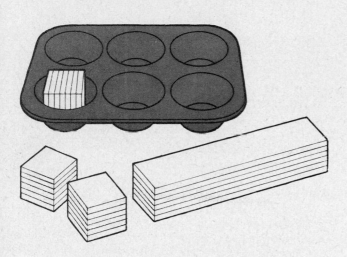

Crescent Rolls: Makes 16 or 24 rolls.

¼ recipe Favorite Yeast Rolls
2 tablespoons butter or margarine, melted

Divide dough in half; roll out each half on a lightly floured surface to an 8-inch round; cut into 8 or 12 wedges. Brush wedges with melted butter. Roll up each wedge, starting at the large end; place, pointed-side down on an ungreased cooky sheet, curving the ends of the rolls slightly in order to shape as crescents.

Knots: Makes 16 rolls.

¼ recipe Favorite Yeast Rolls

Divide dough into 16 equal pieces. Roll each piece with palms of hands to a 6-inch rope on lightly floured surface. Tie a simple knot; form a loop; bring one end through. Place knots on greased cooky sheet 2 inches apart.

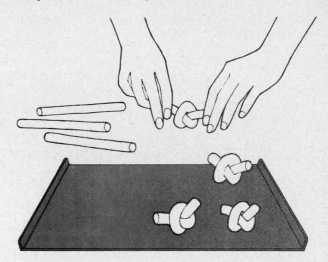

Cloverleaf Rolls: Makes 12 rolls.

¼ recipe Favorite Yeast Rolls
2 tablespoons butter or margarine, melted

Divide dough into quarters and divide each quarter into 9 pieces to make 36 small pieces of dough. Shape dough into marble-size balls and place, 3 at a time, into greased muffin-pan cups; brush generously with butter.

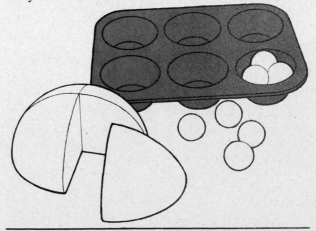

SPECIAL TIPS: To serve frozen baked yeast rolls, place on a cooky sheet and heat in a slow oven (300°) 15 minutes, or just until hot.
• To freshen and reheat rolls that aren't frozen, place in a large brown paper bag; sprinkle bag with a few drops of water; close tightly. Heat in moderate oven (350°) 10 minutes.

*Make our basic Danish Pastry
dough and create this lovely
Mayor's Braid, plus
a dozen of the beautiful
individual pastries shown
on page 39. Recipes
for all in this
chapter.*

Butter-melting Blueberry Muffins from a
bountiful basket. Also shown: Corn
Muffins and Whole Wheat Muffins. Recipes
in this chapter.

3

QUICK BREADS

If you've wanted to bake butter-melting biscuits, mouth-watering muffins, or tempting tea loaves, but didn't think you had the time, rejoice! The quickest of Quick Breads are in this chapter, including the beauty on our cover—Classic Strawberry Shortcake.

Swirls of frosting and glistening bits of candied orange peel add the finishing touches to the best Orange-Nut Cake ever created! Recipe in this chapter.

Photographer: George Nordhausen

4

CAKES AND FROSTINGS

Bake our basic butter, white or chocolate cake, add a fabulous frosting and a great garnish, and you can create any of dozens of simply sensational cakes. And that's not all! You'll find dozens more cake recipes in this chapter, plus an entire section on cake decorating.

BUTTER AND POUND CAKES

SPECIAL TIPS: Here are some helpful hints to make your cake—and cupcake—baking a snap:

• When making a cake, *never* use vegetable oil or melted shortening unless the recipe specifically calls for it; otherwise, your cake will turn out heavy and tough, and may sink in the middle.

• The easiest way to tell if a cake is done is to touch it lightly in the center. If it springs back, it's done. Another test is to insert a wooden pick in the center of the cake. If batter or crumbs cling to the pick, bake cake for an additional five minutes; then test it again.

• Always leave cakes in pans on wire racks for at least 10 minutes, to cool. Then loosen sides with a knife or spatula, invert each cake on wire rack or plate, and *immediately* turn cake right side up on wire rack to complete cooling.

• Most butter cake recipes will make between 24 and 36 medium-size cupcakes. To make cupcakes, place pleated muffin-pan liners in muffin-pan cups. Fill each ⅔ full with batter. Bake in a moderate oven (375°) 20 minutes, or until centers spring back when lightly pressed with fingertip.

Basic Recipe

GOLDEN BUTTER CAKE

Here's a basic double-layer yellow cake to be filled or frosted with any filling or frosting you choose. The possibilities are almost limitless!

Bake at 350° for 30 minutes.
Makes two 9-inch layers, or about 24 cupcakes.

   3 cups <u>sifted</u> cake flour
2½ teaspoons baking powder
  ½ teaspoon salt
  ¾ cup (1½ sticks) butter or margarine, softened
1⅔ cups sugar
   2 eggs
   2 teaspoons vanilla
1⅓ cups milk

1. Grease two 9x1½-inch round layer-cake pans. Dust lightly with flour; tap out excess.
2. Sift flour, baking powder and salt onto wax paper.
3. Beat butter or margarine, sugar, eggs and vanilla in a large bowl with electric mixer at high speed, 3 minutes. (Finish mixing cake by hand.)
4. Add flour mixture alternately with milk, beating after each addition until batter is smooth. Pour into prepared pans.
5. Bake in a moderate oven (350°) 30 minutes, or until centers of layers spring back when lightly pressed with fingertip.

6. Cool layers in pans on wire racks 10 minutes. Loosen around edges with knife; turn out onto wire racks; cool completely.
7. Put layers together with CHOCOLATE BUTTER CREAM FROSTING, BURNT SUGAR FROSTING, or any frosting you prefer. Make any of the frosting patterns shown on page 77, or try your hand at one of the easy-to-make garnishes shown on pages 76 through 78.

BANANA-NUT CAKE

The cake layers have nuts baked inside. The finished, frosted cake has nuts outside; there's banana through and through!

Bake at 350° for 30 minutes.
Makes one 9-inch double-layer cake.

2⅓ cups <u>sifted</u> cake flour
2½ teaspoons baking powder
  ½ teaspoon baking soda
  ½ teaspoon salt
  ½ teaspoon ground cinnamon
   1 cup mashed ripe bananas (2 medium-size)
  ½ cup buttermilk
  ½ cup (1 stick) butter or margarine
1¼ cups sugar
   2 eggs
  ¼ teaspoon vanilla
  ¾ cup chopped walnuts
     Rum Butter Cream Frosting (recipe page 73)

1. Grease two 9x1½-inch round layer-cake pans; dust lightly with flour; tap out excess.
2. Sift flour, baking powder, baking soda, salt, and cinnamon onto wax paper. Stir buttermilk into mashed bananas in a small bowl.
3. Beat butter or margarine, sugar, and eggs in large bowl with electric mixer at high speed, 3 minutes. (Finish mixing cake by hand.)
4. Stir in flour mixture alternately with banana-milk mixture, beating after each addition until batter is smooth. Stir in the ¼ teaspoon vanilla and ¼ cup of the chopped nuts; pour the cake batter into prepared pans.
5. Bake in moderate oven (350°) 30 minutes, or until centers spring back when lightly pressed with fingertip.
6. Cool layers in pans on wire racks 10 minutes; loosen around edges with a knife; turn out onto wire racks; cool completely.
7. Put layers together with RUM BUTTER CREAM FROSTING; frost side and top with remaining frosting. Press remaining ½ cup chopped nuts on sides of cake. Garnish top of cake with banana slices, if you wish. (Dip slices in orange or pineapple juice to keep them white.)

Chocolate Chip Cookies with an
extra special crunch—chopped walnuts.
Recipe in this chapter.

Photographer: George Nordhausen

5

COOKIES

Bake a batch of the best cookies ever! Choose crisp, crunchy drop cookies, chewy bar cookies or pretty rolled or molded and pressed cookies. They're all in this chapter—along with an extra bonus for you—a baker's dozen of easy-to-trace cooky cutter patterns!

SCOTCH SHORTBREAD

Crispy butter cookies to sprinkle with colored sugar.

Bake at 325° for 20 minutes.
Makes about 5 dozen cookies.

    1 cup (2 sticks) butter or margarine
    ½ cup superfine granulated sugar
    1 teaspoon vanilla
    2¼ cups sifted all purpose flour

1. Beat butter or margarine with sugar in a large bowl, until light and fluffy; beat in vanilla.
2. Stir in flour, one third at a time, blending well to make a stiff dough. Knead 10 to 15 minutes, or until smooth. Chill several hours, or overnight, until firm enough to handle.
3. Roll or pat out dough, on a lightly floured surface, one quarter at a time, to a ¼-inch thickness. Cut into small rounds with a 1½-inch cutter. Place cookies, 1 inch apart, on large cooky sheets. Reroll and cut out all trimmings.
4. Bake in a slow oven (325°) 20 minutes, or until firm, but not brown. Remove from cooky sheet to wire racks; cool completely.

ALMOND-FILLED PASTRY CRESCENTS

From Morocco come these melt-in-your-mouth "Kab et Ghzal" (or Gazelle Horns).

Bake at 400° for 12 minutes.
Makes about 4 dozen cookies.

    2¼ cups sifted all-purpose flour
    ½ teaspoon salt
    1 cup (2 sticks) butter or margarine
    4 tablespoons ice water
    1 can (8 ounces) almond paste
    2 tablespoons granulated sugar
    1 egg
    ⅓ cup almonds, ground
    ⅔ cup 10X (confectioners') sugar

1. Combine flour and salt in a medium-size bowl. Cut in butter or margarine with a pastry blender until mixture is crumbly. Add ice water, one tablespoon at a time; combine with a fork until moistened.
2. Shape pastry into a ball; divide into 3 equal pieces; shape each piece into a round; flatten slightly. Wrap each third in plastic wrap. Refrigerate at least 1 hour.
3. Place almond paste in a small bowl; break up with a fork. Beat in egg, the 2 tablespoons of granulated sugar and ground almonds until mixture is thoroughly combined. (Mixture will be sticky.)
4. Turn almond mixture out onto a lightly floured surface. Shape into a ball with floured hands. Divide into thirds. Shape each third into a rope ½-inch in diameter and 16 inches long. (If mixture sticks, flour hands and surface lightly.) Cut each rope into sixteen 1-inch pieces.
5. Roll out pastry, one third at a time, to a ⅛-inch thickness, on a lightly floured surface; roll to a 12x12-inch square. Trim off rough edges. With a sharp knife, cut into sixteen 3-inch squares.
6. Place one piece of almond paste diagonally across one corner of the pastry square. Lift the point over the paste and roll jelly roll fashion. Pinch the ends enclosing the almond filling. Curve the pastry into a crescent.
7. Place crescents, 1 inch apart, on an ungreased cooky sheet. Bake in a hot oven (400°) 12 minutes, or until edges of cookies just *begin* to brown.
8. Place 10X sugar in a pie plate or on large sheet of wax paper. Place warm cookies, a few at a time, upside down in sugar to coat; turn once or twice.
9. Place cookies on wire racks to cool thoroughly. Store in wax paper-separated layers in an airtight tin. Sprinkle with additional sugar before serving.

Low Calorie

32-CALORIE APRICOT PINWHEELS

So delicious, you'll never guess they're dietetic!

Bake at 375° for 12 minutes.
Makes 7 dozen cookies at 32 calories each.

    1 cup apricots, finely chopped
    ½ cup boiling water
    2½ cups sifted all-purpose flour
    ½ teaspoon baking powder
    10 tablespoons butter or margarine, softened
    ¼ cup firmly packed brown sugar
    Sugar substitute to equal 4 tablespoons sugar
    6 tablespoons cold water

1. Combine apricots and boiling water in small bowl; allow to stand until most of water is absorbed. Drain.
2. Sift flour and baking powder into mixing bowl.
3. Beat butter or margarine, brown sugar, sugar substitute and water until well blended; add to flour mixture. Blend with fork until mixture forms a ball.
4. Place dough on wax paper; flatten slightly. Wrap in the wax paper; chill in freezer 20 minutes.
5. Roll out dough on a floured surface to form 24x10-inch rectangle. Spread drained apricots over dough. Roll up dough from the longer side to form a 24-inch long roll; cut in half. Wrap each roll in wax paper. Chill 3 hours or overnight.
6. Cut rolls into ⅜-inch-thick slices. Place on non-stick cooky sheets.
7. Bake in a moderate oven (375°) for 12 minutes. Let the cookies cool on paper toweling.

*Old-fashioned Christmas cookies
to give as gifts or to have on hand
when family and friends stop by.
Top right: molded Springerle.
Center: spicy cut-out Pepparkakor.
Also shown: chocolate-nut-tipped
Spritz Slims and Noel Wreaths.
Recipes in this chapter.*

Country-fresh fruit pies to enjoy any time of the year.
From top left, clockwise: Fresh Latticed Peach Pie,
Nectarine Streusel Pie, Fresh Blueberry Pie,
and Deep-Dish Rhubarb-Strawberry Pie.
Recipes in this chapter.

6

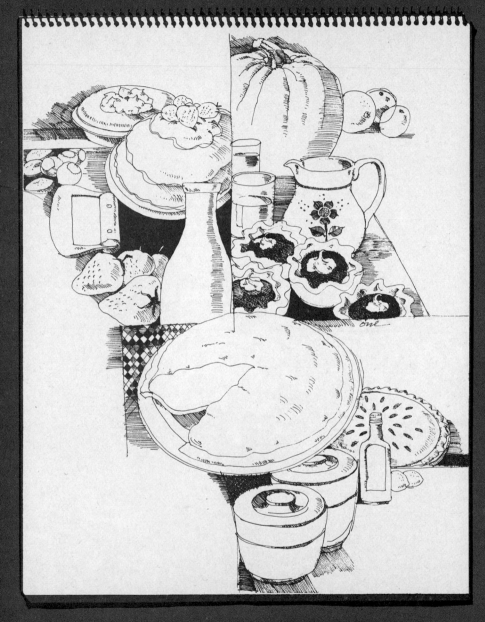

PIES AND TARTS

It's easy to see why pie is such a big favorite. Few desserts are as versatile. A light, golden pastry shell can be filled with a bubbly fruit, a frothy chiffon, a smooth cream, custard or cheese filling. They're all delicious, and they're all in this chapter.

FLAKY PASTRY I

Makes enough for one 9-inch double-crust pie or lattice-top pie.

2 cups <u>sifted</u> all-purpose flour
1 teaspoon salt
⅔ cup vegetable shortening
4 or 5 tablespoons cold water

1. Sift flour and salt into a medium-size bowl; cut in shortening with a fork or pastry blender until mixture is crumbly.
2. Sprinkle water over mixture, 1 tablespoon at a time; mix lightly with a fork just until pastry holds together and leaves sides of bowl clean. Divide dough in half.
3. To make bottom crust, roll out half to a 12-inch round on a lightly floured surface. Fit into a 9-inch pie plate. Trim overhang to ½ inch.
4. To make top crust, roll out remaining pastry to an 11-inch round. Cut several slits or decorator cutouts near the center (to let steam escape).
5. Once pie is filled, place top crust over filling. Trim overhang to ½ inch, even with bottom pastry. Pinch to seal. Turn edge up and in, to seal in juices. Pinch again to make stand-up edge; flute, or try one of the other pie edgings shown on page 105.
6. Bake pie, and cool, following directions in individual recipes.

Lattice Top: For easy-to-follow directions on how to make a lattice top, see page 105.

SPECIAL TIPS: Here are a few pointers to help make your pastry flaky, light and easy to make.
• Handle pastry dough *as little as possible;* unlike bread dough, pastry dough that's overhandled will become tough. As soon as the dough holds together, form a ball; flatten the ball; then roll the dough out to the size specified.
• Always roll pastry dough from the center to the edge. That way, your crust will be even in size and thickness.
• Turn the dough gently as you roll it, to prevent it from sticking.
• For a good size marker, use your pie plate! Turn it upside down on the rolled dough. Then, you can judge how much more rolling to do.
• To help center the pastry dough in your pie plate, fold the rolled pastry in half over your rolling pin; lay one half over the pie plate. When the rolling pin is across the center, flip the other half over the rest of the pie plate.
• Be sure to fit the dough *loosely* in your pie plate. If the dough is stretched taut, it will shrink during baking.
• Trimmings from pastry can be re-rolled, cut and sprinkled with sugar and cinnamon for extra treats.

FLAKY PASTRY II

Make enough for one 9-inch pastry shell, for a single-crust pie.

1½ cups <u>sifted</u> all-purpose flour
1 teaspoon salt
½ cup vegetable shortening
4 tablespoons cold water (about)

1. Sift flour and salt in a medium-size bowl; cut in shortening with a fork or pastry blender, until mixture is crumbly.
2. Sprinkle water over mixture, 1 tablespoon at a time; mix lightly with a fork just until pastry holds together and leaves sides of bowl clean. Make a ball; flatten it.
3. Roll out to a 12-inch round on a lightly floured surface; fit into a 9-inch pie plate. Trim overhang to ½ inch. Turn edge under. Pinch to make a stand-up edge; flute, or try one of the other decorative pie edgings shown on page 105.

For baked pastry shells: Prick shell well all over with a fork. Bake in a very hot oven (450°) 5 minutes. Look at shell; if bubbles have formed, prick again. (After about 5 minutes of baking, pastry will have set and any bubbles formed will be permanent.) Continue to bake another 10 minutes, or until pastry is golden brown. Cool completely, in pie plate, on a wire rack.

SPECIAL TIPS: There's another way to bake your unfilled pastry shell smooth and bubble-free besides pricking all over with a fork. Fit a piece of foil or wax paper in bottom of plate over pastry; fill the shell with rice or beans (which can be reused); then bake 5 minutes, or until pastry is set. Remove rice or beans and foil or wax paper. Continue to bake until crust is golden brown.
• For lattice pies as well as pastry shells, turn edges of dough *under* and pinch to form a stand-up edge. Reason: There's no need to seal in juices, as there is with most two-crust pies; so the edge can be turned under for a neater appearance.

CRUMB CRUST

Makes one unbaked 9-inch crust.

1⅓ cups graham cracker crumbs (about 18 squares)
¼ cup sugar
¼ cup butter or margarine, softened

1. Mix graham cracker crumbs and sugar in a small bowl; blend in butter or margarine.
2. Press firmly over bottom and side of a buttered 9-inch pie plate; chill while making pie filling.

Vanilla Wafer-Pecan Crumb Crust: Combine 1 cup vanilla wafer crumbs with ½ cup ground pecans and ¼ cup softened butter or margarine in a small bowl. Press firmly over bottom and side of a lightly buttered 9-inch pie plate.

For baked crumb crusts: Bake in a moderate oven (350°) 8 minutes, or until set. Cool completely on a wire rack.

Low Calorie

SLIM-DOWN GRAHAM CRACKER CRUST

Bake at 400° for 5 minutes.
Makes one 9-inch crumb crust.
Total calories: 534.

   3 tablespoons soft diet margarine
   1 cup packaged graham cracker crumbs

1. Blend margarine and crumbs thoroughly, using a fork. Press onto bottom and side of a 9-inch pie plate, covering all surfaces except rim.
2. Bake in hot oven (400°) 5 minutes. Cool before filling.

SOUR CREAM PASTRY FOR TURNOVERS

Makes enough for 12 turnovers.

   3 cups sifted all-purpose flour
   2 tablespoons sugar
   1 cup (2 sticks) butter or margarine
   1 cup dairy sour cream

1. Measure flour and sugar into a medium-size bowl.
2. Cut in butter or margarine with a pastry blender until mixture is crumbly. Add sour cream.
3. Mix lightly with a fork until dough clings together and starts to leave side of bowl. Gather dough together with hands and knead a few times.
4. Wrap dough in plastic wrap or wax paper; chill several hours, or overnight.

COOKY CRUST PASTRY

Makes one 10-inch crust.

   2 cups sifted all-purpose flour
   ½ cup sugar
   ¾ cup (1½ sticks) butter or margarine, softened
   2 egg yolks, slightly beaten
   1 teaspoon vanilla

Mix flour and sugar together in a medium-size bowl; cut in butter or margarine with a pastry blender until mixture is crumbly. Add egg yolks and vanilla; mix lightly with a fork just until pastry holds together and leaves side of bowl clean. Chill until ready to use.

Note: For half the recipe, use 1 cup flour, ¼ cup sugar, 6 tablespoons butter or margarine, 1 egg yolk and ½ teaspoon vanilla.

FRUIT PIES

SPECIAL TIP: How many servings do you get from one pie? It all depends upon the richness. For fruit pies, figure 6 generous servings. For custard, cream and other rich pies, count on 8 servings. And for super-sweets such as Virginia Pecan Pie, smaller portions are usually sufficient.

FRESH LATTICED PEACH PIE

Fresh ripe peach pie with a see-through top. Enjoy this Southern favorite any time.

Bake at 425° for 15 minutes, then at 350° for 40 minutes.
Makes one 9-inch pie with lattice top.

   ½ cup sugar
   2 tablespoons sifted all-purpose flour
   ½ teaspoon ground cinnamon
   ¼ teaspoon salt
   6 ripe peaches (about 3 pounds)
   1 tablespoon lemon juice
   ¼ teaspoon almond extract
   Flaky Pastry I (recipe page 102)
   OR: **1 package piecrust mix**
   2 tablespoons butter or margarine
   Milk or cream
   Sugar

1. Mix sugar, flour, cinnamon and salt together.
2. Drop peaches, 3 or 4 at a time, into boiling water; leave in 15 to 30 seconds; lift out with slotted spoon. Peel off skins; cut in half; remove pits, then slice (you should have 10 cups).
3. Place peaches in a large bowl; sprinkle with lemon juice and almond extract; toss lightly. Sprinkle with sugar mixture; toss gently to mix.
4. Prepare pastry. Spoon filling into bottom crust; dot with butter. Cover with lattice top (for easy directions, see page 105). Brush lattice top with milk or cream and sprinkle with sugar.
5. Bake in a hot oven (425°) 15 minutes; then lower heat to 350°; continue to bake 35 to 40 minutes longer, or until pastry is golden and juices bubble up near center. Cool on wire rack 1 hour.

5. Beat egg whites until stiff peaks form (use a non-plastic bowl). Measure ice water, remaining 1 tablespoon of lemon juice and nonfat dry milk powder into small bowl. Beat with electric mixer at high speed until mixture is the consistency of stiffly whipped cream, about 8 to 10 minutes.

6. Fold the beaten egg whites and whipped nonfat dry milk into gelatin mixture; turn into cooled pie shell. Refrigerate about 4 hours, or until set.

PEACH MELBA CHIFFON PIE

This spectacular looking pie combines all of the features of luscious Peach Melba—creamy filling, raspberry sauce, peach slices on top!

Makes one 9-inch single-crust pie.

> **Flaky Pastry II (recipe page 102)**
> OR: **½ package piecrust mix**
> 1 **can (1 pound, 14 ounces) sliced peaches, drained**
> ¾ **cup sugar (for filling)**
> 2 **envelopes unflavored gelatin**
> 4 **eggs, separated**
> ⅔ **cup milk**
> 1 **package (10 ounces) frozen raspberries, thawed**
> 1 **tablespoon cornstarch**
> 1 **tablespoon sugar (for topping)**
> ½ **cup frozen whipped topping, thawed (from a 4-ounce container)**

1. Prepare *baked* pastry shell.
2. Chop peaches very fine, saving 6 slices for top.
3. Combine ½ cup of the sugar and gelatin in a medium-size saucepan; beat egg yolks with milk in a small bowl; stir into gelatin mixture. (Save egg whites and remaining ¼ cup sugar for Step 5.)
4. Cook gelatin mixture over low heat, stirring constantly, about 10 minutes, or until mixture coats a spoon. Cool slightly; stir in peaches. Place pan in a bowl of ice and water to speed setting; chill, stirring often, until mixture starts to thicken.
5. While peach mixture chills, beat egg whites in a medium-size bowl until foamy white; slowly beat in remaining ¼ cup sugar until meringue stands in firm peaks. Fold meringue into peach mixture until no streaks of white remain. Spoon into cooled pastry shell. Chill at least 2 hours, or until set.
6. Drain raspberries; reserve syrup. In a small saucepan, combine ½ cup syrup, cornstarch and 1 tablespoon sugar. Cook, stirring constantly, until mixture thickens and comes to a boil; let bubble 1 minute. Cool, then combine with raspberries. Spoon over top of pie, leaving about a 2-inch border all around. Refrigerate about 1 hour longer.
7. Just before serving, spoon the whipped topping in the center of the pie. Place reserved peaches around the topping, pinwheel fashion.

CUSTARD AND CREAM PIES

COCONUT CUSTARD PIE

One of America's favorite pies—crunchy coconut and vanilla in a smooth custard filling.

Bake shell at 425° for 5 minutes, then bake pie at 325° for 40 minutes.
Makes one 9-inch single-crust pie.

> **Flaky Pastry II (recipe page 102)**
> OR: **½ package piecrust mix**
> 3 **cups milk**
> 4 **eggs**
> ⅓ **cup sugar**
> ¼ **teaspoon salt**
> 1 **can (3½ ounces) flaked coconut**
> 1 **teaspoon vanilla**

1. Prepare *unbaked* pastry shell.
2. Bake in a hot oven (425°) 5 minutes. Remove shell; cool; lower oven temperature to 325°.
3. In a medium-size saucepan, heat milk slowly until bubbles appear around edge.
4. In a large bowl, beat eggs slightly; stir in sugar and salt; slowly stir in milk. Strain into another bowl; stir in coconut and vanilla. Pour into partly baked pastry shell.
5. Bake in a slow oven (325°) 40 minutes, or until center is almost set, but still soft. (Do not overbake; custard will set as it cools.) Cool on a wire rack. Serve warm or chilled.

VIRGINIA PECAN PIE

This Southern treat is luscious and rich. Serve it in small portions with a drift of softly whipped cream.

Bake at 350° for 45 minutes.
Makes one 9-inch single-crust pie.

> **Flaky Pastry II (recipe page 102)**
> OR: **½ package piecrust mix**
> 3 **eggs**
> ½ **cup sugar**
> ½ **teaspoon salt**
> 1 **cup dark corn syrup**
> ¼ **cup butter or margarine, melted**
> 1 **teaspoon vanilla**
> 1 **cup pecan halves**
> 1 **cup heavy cream, whipped**

1. Prepare *unbaked* pastry shell.
2. Beat eggs slightly in a medium-size bowl; blend in sugar, salt, corn syrup, butter or margarine and vanilla. Pour into prepared shell; arrange pecan

Lemon desserts—always refreshing, whether simple or elegant. Shown here, from top down: Lemon-Date Torte (recipe, Chapter 7); Lemon Meringue Pie (recipe, this chapter); and Lemon Pound Cake (recipe, Chapter 4).

3. Place tart shells in jelly roll pan; spoon filling into each one.
4. Bake in a very hot oven (450°) 10 minutes. Lower heat to 350°; bake 25 minutes longer, or until filling is firm. Remove tarts from oven; cool on wire rack.
5. Carefully remove each tart from its pan. Serve topped with sour cream and garnish with walnut halves, if you wish.

SPECIAL TIP: For best results, don't remove cooled tarts from their pans until you're actually ready to serve them. For easy removal, gently hold the edge of each tart with one hand. With the other hand, use a small paring knife and very carefully lift the tart from the pan.

LEMON TARTLETS VERONIQUE

Cookylike shells hold mellow lemon filling—with glazed grapes on top. Pretty fruits to use another time: Strawberries, peach slices.

Bake shells at 375° for 22 minutes.
Makes one dozen 3-inch tarts.

    2 cups <u>sifted</u> all-purpose flour
    3 tablespoons sugar
    ½ teaspoon salt
    ½ cup (1 stick) butter or margarine
    ¼ cup shortening
    6 tablespoons water
      Lemon filling (recipe follows)
    1 pound seedless green grapes, stemmed
      and halved
    1 cup apple jelly, melted and cooled
    1 cup heavy cream

1. Sift flour, sugar and salt into a medium-size bowl. Cut in butter or margarine and shortening with a pastry blender until mixture is crumbly.
2. Sprinkle water over top; mix lightly with a fork until pastry holds together and leaves side of bowl clean. Turn out onto a lightly floured surface; knead just until smooth; divide dough into 12 even pieces. Chill dough 1 hour for easier handling.
3. Press each piece of dough into a 3-inch metal or foil tart-shell pan; cover bottom and side evenly. Fit a small piece of wax paper over pastry in each pan; pour uncooked rice or beans on top to hold pastry in place during baking. Set pans in a large shallow pan for easy handling.
4. Bake in a moderate oven (375°) 10 minutes; remove from oven. Lift out beans or rice and wax paper; return pans to oven. Bake 12 minutes longer, or until pastry is golden. Cool shells completely, in their pans, on wire racks.

5. Spoon LEMON FILLING into each shell; arrange grape halves, cut side up, on top, to form rosettes; brush grapes with apple jelly; chill.
6. Just before serving, beat cream in a medium-size bowl, until stiff. Attach a fancy tip to a pastry bag; fill bag with whipped cream; press out tiny rosettes on top of tartlets. (For directions on how to make your own disposable decorating bag, see page 13.) Chill until serving time.

Lemon Filling: Beat 6 eggs slightly in the top of a large double boiler; stir in 1 cup sugar, ½ cup (1 stick) butter or margarine, 2 teaspoons grated lemon rind, and ⅓ cup lemon juice. Cook, stirring, constantly, over hot, not boiling water, 15 minutes, or until very thick. Pour into a medium-size bowl; cover bowl with plastic wrap; chill until ready to use. Makes 3 cups.

PEACH DUMPLINGS

Luscious peaches, wrapped in flaky, light pastry. An old-fashioned dessert your family will love.

Bake at 425° for 30 minutes.
Makes 6 dumplings.

    ¾ cup water
    ½ cup granulated sugar (for syrup)
    ½ cup bottled grenadine syrup
      Flaky Pastry II (recipe page 102)
      OR: 1 package piecrust mix
    ¼ cup firmly packed brown sugar
    ¼ teaspoon ground cinnamon
    1 tablespoon butter or margarine
    6 large peaches, peeled, halved and pitted
      Milk or cream
      Granulated sugar (for topping)

1. Combine water, the ½ cup granulated sugar, and grenadine syrup in a medium-size saucepan. Heat to boiling, then simmer 5 minutes; remove from heat.
2. Prepare pastry. Roll out on a lightly floured surface to an 18x12-inch rectangle; cut into six 6x6-inch squares.
3. Blend brown sugar, cinnamon and butter or margarine in a small bowl. Spoon into hollows in peach halves; press 2 halves back together.
4. Place a filled peach in center of each pastry square; fold pastry up and around fruit; pinch edges to seal. Place in a 13x9x2-inch baking pan. Brush dumplings lightly with milk or cream; sprinkle with granulated sugar.
5. Bake in a hot oven (425°) 30 minutes, or until pastry is golden and peaches are tender. (Test fruit with a long thin metal skewer.)
6. Cool slightly in pan on a wire rack. Serve warm, with cream or ice cream, if you wish.

Custard and cream pies—favorites from all
sections of the country. Clockwise, from left:
Virginia Pecan Pie, New England Pumpkin-Nut
Pie and Hawaiian Coconut Cream Pie. Recipes
for all are in this chapter.

Sliced nuts and meringue between the layers give this Almond Blitz Torte interesting texture—as well as delicate flavor. Recipe in this chapter.

7

SPECIALTIES

Our "Specialties" chapter is filled with spectacular desserts; luscious,
fruit-filled strudel, rich cream puffs and eclairs, creamy cheesecakes,
elegant tortes and a selection of delicately baked meringues. They're
all so good, you won't know which to try first.

CREAM HORNS PARISIENNE

This simplified version of puff pastry takes very little time and effort, yet it becomes a most elegant dessert, when completed.

Bake at 400° for 20 minutes.
Makes sixteen 5-inch horns.

    3 cups <u>sifted</u> all-purpose flour
 1½ cups (3 sticks) butter or margarine
    1 cup dairy sour cream
       Water
       Sugar
       Pink Cream Filling (recipe follows)

1. Measure flour into a medium-size bowl. Cut in butter or margarine with a pastry blender until mixture is crumbly; add sour cream. Knead lightly with hands just until pastry holds together and leaves side of bowl clean. Wrap dough in wax paper; chill overnight.
2. To make your own cream horn molds: Tear off eight 9-inch pieces heavy-duty foil from an 18-inch-wide roll. Cut each piece in half to make a square; Fold each square crosswise to make a triangle. Using center of longest side of triangle as tip of cone, start at one side and roll up to form a slim cone. (Fold tip down to secure the mold, or fasten with paper clip.)
3. Divide pastry in half. Keep one half refrigerated until ready to use. Roll out evenly to an 18x10-inch rectangle on floured surface. Cut pastry lengthwise into 8 strips, each 1¼ inches wide.
4. Moisten each strip lightly with water. Starting at pointed end, wrap around cone-shaped foil, overlapping slightly. Place on ungreased cooky sheet. Chill 30 minutes; brush each horn with water; sprinkle with sugar.
5. Bake in hot oven (400°) 20 minutes or until puffed and a rich brown color.
6. Remove horns to wire rack to cool. As each horn is cool enough to handle, carefully remove from mold. Cool completely before filling. Use same molds for baking second half of pastry.
7. Fill horns just before serving.

Pink Cream Filling: Beat 2 cups heavy cream, 2 tablespoons sugar and ½ teaspoon almond extract in medium-size bowl, until stiff. Fold in 2 tablespoons finely chopped maraschino cherries and 2 teaspoons syrup from cherries. Add a drop of red food coloring. Makes enough to fill 16 horns.

Note: If you wish to make only 8 horns, use only ½ of filling recipe. Shape second half of horns on molds. Place in a single layer in a pan; freeze. When frozen, wrap in foil or plastic wrap. When ready to use, fill horns and bake as directed. No need to defrost horns before baking them.

Basic Recipe

CREAM PUFF PASTE (Paté à Chou)

This recipe makes 12 large cream puffs or 12 large eclairs or 2 Viennese Mocha-Nut Crowns.

    1 cup water
    ½ cup (1 stick) butter or margarine
    ¼ teaspoon salt
    1 cup <u>sifted</u> all-purpose flour
    4 eggs

1. Heat water, butter or margarine and salt to a full rolling boil in a large saucepan.
2. Add flour all at once. Stir vigorously with a wooden spoon until mixture forms a thick, smooth ball that leaves the side of pan clean (about 1 minute). Remove from heat; cool slightly.
3. Add eggs, one at a time, beating well after each addition, until paste is shiny and smooth. (Paste will separate as you add each egg, but with continued beating, it will smooth out.)
4. Shape, following recipe instructions.

VIENNESE MOCHA-NUT CROWN

A regal dessert that would have pleased the Emperor Franz Joseph himself; truly a royal treat.

Bake at 400° for 40 minutes.
Makes one ring; 6 servings.

 ½ recipe Basic Cream Puff Paste (recipe above)

Chocolate Praline Filling:
 ½ cup hazelnuts or almonds, unblanched
 ⅓ cup granulated sugar
  2 cups heavy cream
 ⅓ cup unsweetened cocoa
 ½ cup 10X (confectioners') sugar

    Chocolate Glaze (recipe follows)
    Coffee Butter Cream (recipe follows)

1. Make BASIC CREAM PUFF PASTE. Draw a 7-inch circle on an ungreased cooky sheet. Spoon paste in 6 mounds, just inside circle. Or, press paste through a pastry bag. Puffs should almost touch.
2. Bake in a hot oven (400°) 40 minutes, or until puffed and golden brown. With a small knife, make slits in ring to let steam escape. Turn off heat; leave ring in oven 5 minutes longer. Remove to wire rack, then cool completely.
3. Make CHOCOLATE PRALINE FILLING: Combine nuts, sugar and water in a small heavy skillet. Bring to a boil, stirring constantly. Boil rapidly, uncovered, until nuts make a popping sound, about 10

*This regal Viennese Mocha-Nut Crown pulls
apart into six perfect chocolate cream
puffs. Recipe in this chapter.*

The moist fruit filling and flaky-light pastry make this Apple-Nut Strudel a sensational dessert. Recipe in this chapter.

Combine butter or margarine and chocolate in a small bowl. Beat until thoroughly blended. Add sugar alternately with sour cream and vanilla, beating until mixture is spreadable.

Chocolate Rum Glaze: Combine 1 square semisweet chocolate, 1 tablespoon butter or margarine, 1 tablespoon 10X (confectioners') sugar and 1 tablespoon rum or brandy in a small bowl; set bowl in a small saucepan partly filled with water. Heat, stirring often, until chocolate is melted; cool slightly. If glaze separates, add a few drops of cold water or milk; then stir until it is smooth.

LEMON-DATE TORTE

There are chopped dates and walnuts in the delicate layers of this torte, and smooth lemon filling between. A dollop of whipped cream and a pretty lemon rose on top make the perfect garnish.

Bake at 350° for 40 minutes.
Makes one 8-inch cake.

1½ cups <u>sifted</u> all-purpose flour
1½ teaspoons baking powder
 ½ teaspoon ground cinnamon
 ¼ teaspoon salt
 ⅛ teaspoon ground cloves
 1 package (8 ounces) pitted dates, chopped
 ½ cup walnuts, chopped
 4 eggs, separated
 1 cup sugar
 5 tablespoons butter or margarine
 1 teaspoon vanilla
 ⅓ cup milk
   Lemon Filling (recipe page 74)

1. Grease two 8x1½-inch round layer-cake pans; dust with flour; tap out excess.
2. Sift flour, baking powder, cinnamon, salt and cloves into a large bowl; stir in dates and walnuts.
3. Beat egg whites in a medium-size bowl until foamy white and double in volume. Gradually beat in ½ cup of the sugar, 1 tablespoon at a time, until sugar dissolves, and meringue stands in firm peaks.
4. Beat butter or margarine with remaining ½ cup sugar in a large bowl; beat in 2 of the egg yolks and vanilla until light and fluffy. Beat in flour mixture, one half at a time, alternately with milk, until blended; fold in meringue. Spread evenly into prepared pans.
5. Bake in a moderate oven (350°) 40 minutes, or until centers spring back when lightly pressed with fingertip. Cool in pans on wire racks 10 minutes. Turn out onto racks; cool completely.
6. Prepare LEMON FILLING. (Use remaining 2 yolks from torte recipe.)

7. Split cake layers to make 4 thin layers; spread each of 3 layers with ⅓ cup of the LEMON FILLING; stack together on a serving plate. Top with plain layer. Garnish with whipped cream and a lemon rose (directions page 78). Chill at least 4 hours to mellow. Cut in thin wedges.

ALMOND BLITZ TORTE

A light-as-air torte featuring frothy meringue, almonds and whipped cream between the layers.

Bake at 350° for 30 minutes.
Makes one 9-inch cake.

 2 cups <u>sifted</u> cake flour
 2 teaspoons baking powder
 1 teaspoon salt
 5 eggs, separated
1¾ cups sugar
 ⅓ cup vegetable shortening
 1 teaspoon vanilla
 ½ teaspoon almond extract
 ½ cup milk
 ¾ cup almonds, sliced
 1 cup heavy cream
 2 tablespoons sugar

1. Grease two 9x1½-inch layer-cake pans; dust with flour; tap out excess.
2. Sift flour, baking powder and salt onto wax paper; reserve.
3. Beat egg whites in small bowl with electric mixer at high speed until foamy white and double in volume. Gradually beat in ¾ cup of the sugar, until meringue stands in firm peaks; reserve.
4. With same beater (don't wash) beat remaining 1 cup sugar, shortening, egg yolks, vanilla and almond extract in large bowl with electric mixer at high speed, 3 minutes.
5. Stir in flour mixture by hand, alternately with milk, beating after each addition, until batter is smooth. Spread into pans. Carefully spread reserved meringue over batter; sprinkle with almonds.
6. Bake in moderate oven (350°) 30 minutes, or until meringue is golden brown and cake begins to pull from sides of pan. (Meringue may crack in baking, but don't worry, it will settle while cooling).
7. Cool cake layers in pans on wire rack 30 minutes. or until cool enough to handle. Loosen around edges with a knife; turn out onto your hand, then gently place, meringue sides up, on wire racks; cool.
8. At least 2 hours before serving, beat cream and 2 tablespoons sugar in a small bowl, until stiff.
9. Put layers together on serving plate with part of the whipped cream; decorate top of cake with remaining cream and garnish with strawberries, if you wish. Refrigerate until serving time.

can be done several days before serving; simply store meringue shell in an airtight container.

8. One hour before serving: Place meringue shell on a serving plate. Scoop ice cream with large spoon to make "petals" and fill meringue shell. Arrange peach halves over ice cream; top with ALMOND PEACH GLAZE.

Almond Peach Glaze: Mash 1 peeled, halved, and pitted ripe peach in a small saucepan; stir in ½ cup light corn syrup. Heat to boiling; lower heat; simmer 5 minutes. Remove from heat; stir in ½ teaspoon almond extract. Cool. Makes about 1 cup.

LEMON ANGEL PIE

This is a make-ahead dessert. It needs long chilling to mellow to perfection.

Bake shell at 275° for 1 hour.
Makes one 9-inch pie.

  Butter or margarine
  4 **eggs, separated**
  ¼ **teaspoon cream of tartar**
  ½ **teaspoon salt**
  ½ **teaspoon vanilla**
  2 **cups sugar**
  4 **tablespoons cornstarch**
  1½ **cups water**
  ½ **cup lemon juice**
  2 **tablespoons butter or margarine**
  1 **cup heavy cream**

1. Generously butter a 9-inch pie plate.
2. Beat egg whites with cream of tartar, ¼ teaspoon of the salt and vanilla in a large bowl, until foamy white and double in volume. Using an electric mixer, gradually beat in 1 cup of the sugar, until sugar dissolves completely and meringue stands in stiff peaks (about 25 minutes).
3. Spoon meringue into pie plate. Spread almost to side of plate, hollowing center and building up edge slightly to form a shell.
4. Bake in a very slow oven (275°) 1 hour, or until firm and lightly golden. Cool completely in pie plate on wire rack.
5. While shell bakes, mix remaining 1 cup sugar, cornstarch, and ¼ teaspoon salt in a medium-size saucepan. Stir in water, then beat in egg yolks and lemon juice.
6. Cook, stirring constantly, until mixture thickens, and boils, 3 minutes; remove from heat. Stir in butter or margarine, until melted; pour into medium-size bowl; cover. Chill until completely cold.
7. Beat cream in a medium-size bowl until stiff. Layer lemon filling, alternately with whipped cream, into meringue shell. Chill about 5 hours, or overnight, before cutting.

RASPBERRY MERINGUE CAKE

A towering beauty—five meringue layers are stacked with raspberry cream and topped with fresh berries. A super dessert!

Bake shells at 300° for 30 minutes.
Makes one 10-inch meringue.

  6 **egg whites**
  ¼ **teaspoon cream of tartar**
  1½ **cups sugar (for meringue)**
  ½ **cup almonds, ground**
  ½ **cup cornstarch**
  ¼ **cup red raspberry jelly**
  2 **cups heavy cream**
  1 **tablespoon sugar (for cream)**
  Fresh red raspberries

1. Grease 2 large and 1 small cooky sheets. Dust with flour; tap out excess. Using an 8-inch round layer-cake pan as a guide, draw 2 circles on each of the large cooky sheets and 1 on the smaller one. Set aside for Step 3. (If you do not have enough cooky sheets or oven space to bake all of the meringue layers at once, shape meringues on greased, floured foil, and let stand at room temperature until first batch is baked. Then simply slide foil onto cooky sheets.
2. Beat egg whites with cream of tartar in a large bowl with an electric mixer until foamy white and double in volume. Gradually add the 1½ cups sugar, 1 tablespoon at a time, beating all the time, until sugar dissolves and meringue stands in firm peaks (about 25 minutes).
3. Mix almonds and cornstarch in a small bowl; fold into meringue until completely blended. Spoon meringue evenly into the five circles; spread out to the edges.
4. Bake in a slow oven (300°) 30 minutes, or until layers are firm and lightly golden. Cool 5 minutes on cooky sheets on wire racks, then loosen meringues carefully with a wide spatula, and slide onto racks; cool completely.
5. Three hours before serving, whip jelly with a fork, in a cup. Beat 1½ cups of the cream in a medium-size bowl until thick; beat in jelly; continue beating until stiff.
6. Place 1 meringue layer on a serving plate; spread with one-fourth of the cream mixture; repeat with remaining layers and cream, leaving top layer plain.
7. Beat remaining ½ cup cream with the 1 tablespoon sugar in a small bowl until stiff; spoon in puffs on top layer; garnish with red raspberries. Chill until serving time. To serve, cut in wedges. *Note:* If meringues are made a day ahead, stack layers with wax paper between them, and store in a cool, dry place.

Whether you're giving a lavish dinner party or just having a few friends over for a casual evening of cards and games, you're sure to delight your guests with this fantastic Chocolate Walnut Torte. Recipe in this chapter.

Peaches, pineapple, grapes, strawberries—choose any fruit you wish. They're all beautiful and delicious when glazed atop our Easy Cheese Fruit Tarts. Recipe in this chapter.

8

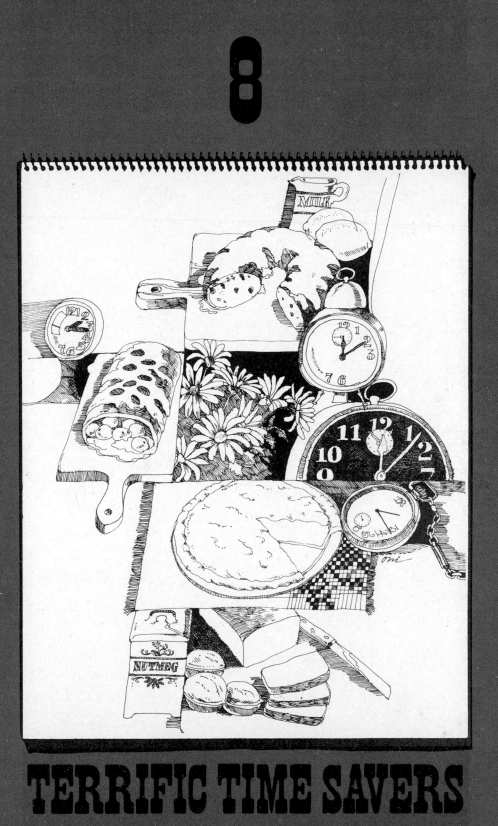

TERRIFIC TIME SAVERS

Even when time is short, you can still turn out delicious cakes and pastries. The trick is to use convenience foods and cut preparation time to a minimum. In this chapter you'll see how to do it, and how to create sensational baked desserts in almost no time at all.

CAKES, CUPCAKES AND PASTRY

WALNUT COFFEE CAKE

Refrigerated rolls make a quick coffee cake, when butter, cinnamon, brown sugar and nuts are rolled up inside, and the crescents are placed in layers.

Bake at 375° for 35 minutes.
Makes one 9x5x3-inch coffee cake.

- **2 packages refrigerated crescent dinner rolls**
- **2 tablespoons butter or margarine, softened**
- **½ cup firmly packed brown sugar**
- **2 teaspoons ground cinnamon**
- **¼ cup chopped walnuts**

1. Unroll dough; separate into triangles. Spread each triangle with part of the butter or margarine.
2. Combine brown sugar, cinnamon and walnuts in a small bowl. Sprinkle about 1 tablespoon of the mixture over each dough triangle. Roll up as label directs.
3. Place rolls, point sides down, in a greased 9x5x3-inch pan, in two layers. Brush top of loaf with remaining butter or margarine; sprinkle with remaining topping.
4. Bake in moderate oven (375°) 35 minutes, or until golden brown. Turn cake out onto wire rack; cool completely before serving.

ISLANDS BANANA CAKE

Ripe bananas and tender coconut in a buttery topping—poured over yellow cake, then quick-broiled for a yummy warm dessert.

Bake at 350° for 30 minutes.
Makes one 13x9x2-inch cake.

- **2 cups biscuit mix**
- **½ cup granulated sugar**
- **½ teaspoon ground mace**
- **2 eggs**
- **½ cup milk**
- **1 teaspoon vanilla**
- **6 tablespoons (¾ stick) butter or margarine**
- **¼ cup firmly packed brown sugar**
- **½ cup flaked coconut**
- **½ cup chopped walnuts**
- **3 medium-size ripe bananas**

1. Combine biscuit mix, granulated sugar, mace, eggs, milk, vanilla and 3 tablespoons of the butter or margarine in a large bowl. Beat with electric mixer at low speed ½ minute to blend ingredients.

Increase speed to medium-high; beat 4 minutes. Scrape side of bowl often with rubber spatula.
2. Turn batter into a buttered 13x9x2-inch baking pan; spread evenly.
3. Bake in a moderate oven (350°) 30 minutes, or until center of cake springs back when lightly pressed with fingertip. Cool cake a few minutes on wire rack.
4. Set oven temperature to broil.
5. Combine brown sugar and remaining 3 tablespoons butter or margarine in a small bowl; stir in coconut and walnuts.
6. Peel bananas; slice diagonally and arrange petal fashion, overlapping, on top of cake. Sprinkle with brown sugar mixture.
7. Broil, with top 3 inches from heat, just until topping is bubbly and lightly browned, about 2 minutes (watch cake carefully while browning). Cool cake on wire rack. Cut into squares while still warm.

ORANGE SWEET CAKE

Orange juice and rind provide the tangy taste in this easy cake; walnuts add the crunch, and biscuit mix makes it simple!

Bake at 350° for 30 minutes.
Makes one 9-inch square cake.

- **2 cups biscuit mix**
- **½ cup granulated sugar**
- **2 eggs**
- **1 tablespoon grated orange rind**
- **½ cup orange juice**
- **6 tablespoons butter or margarine, softened**
- **1 teaspoon vanilla**
- **⅓ cup firmly packed brown sugar**
- **½ cup chopped walnuts**
- **1 tablespoon cream**

1. Combine biscuit mix, granulated sugar, eggs, orange rind, orange juice, vanilla and 3 tablespoons of the butter in a large mixing bowl. Beat at low speed with electric mixer ½ minute to blend ingredients. Increase speed to medium-high; beat 4 minutes. Scrape bowl often with rubber spatula.
2. Turn the batter into a buttered 9x9x2-inch baking pan.
3. Bake in moderate oven (350°) 30 minutes, or until center of cake springs back when lightly pressed with finger. Cool cake a few minutes on a wire rack.
4. Combine brown sugar, chopped walnuts, remaining butter and cream; beat until well mixed. Spread on cake. Broil, with top 3 inches from heat, just until topping is bubbly and lightly browned, about 2 minutes. Cool cake on wire rack. Cut cake in squares. Remaining cake may be covered and stored in the pan.

COCONUT-JELLY CUPCAKES

Fancy cupcakes with colorful cut-out tops.

Bake at 350° for 15 minutes.
Makes 30 cupcakes.

   1 package yellow cake mix
   1 can (16½ ounces) vanilla frosting
   **1 jar (12 ounces) currant, raspberry or straw-
      berry jelly**
      Flaked coconut

1. Line 30 medium-size muffin-pan cups with pleated muffin-pan liners.
2. Prepare cake mix, following label directions. Spoon batter into prepared liners. Bake, following label directions.
3. Remove cupcakes from pans to wire racks. Cool. Leave paper liners on for easy handling.
4. Use a small sharp knife to cut a small cone-shaped piece from the top of each cake. Carefully set pieces aside. Spoon a little vanilla frosting into the hole in each cupcake; replace cone-shaped pieces. Spread entire top of each cupcake with jelly; sprinkle with coconut, pressing slightly into jelly.

QUICK CHERRY STRUDEL

This elegant strudel is surprisingly easy to make.

Preheat oven to 450°; bake at 400° for 25 minutes.
Makes 1 large strudel.

   1 package (10 ounces) frozen patty shells
   1 can (1 pound, 5 ounces) cherry pie filling
   2 teaspoons grated lemon rind
  ¼ cup packaged bread crumbs
   1 tablespoon milk
  ¼ cup sliced unblanched almonds
   2 tablespoons sugar

1. Preheat oven to 450°.
2. Let patty shells soften at room temperature for 20 minutes.
3. Combine cherry pie filling and lemon rind in a small bowl; reserve.
4. On a *well-floured cloth-covered surface,* overlap patty shells in a straight line. Using a *floured stockinette covered* rolling pin, press down onto the patty shells. (*Note:* You may use a floured rolling pin without the stockinette, but flour the rolling pin frequently to prevent the patty shells from sticking.) Roll out from center of patty shells to a 22x16-inch rectangle, being careful not to tear pastry.
5. Sprinkle pastry with bread crumbs.
6. Spoon cherry pie filling down length of pastry closest to you into a 2-inch strip and within 2 inches of ends. Fold in sides; keep filling in.
7. Using the floured cloth, grasp at both ends and gently lift the cloth up and let the strudel roll itself up. Carefully slide onto a cooky sheet, keeping seam side down, and form into a horseshoe shape.
8. Brush top generously with milk; sprinkle almond slices on top, pressing well in order to keep in place. Then sprinkle with sugar.
9. Lower oven heat to (400°); bake 25 minutes or until golden brown; let cool on baking sheet 10 minutes. Serve the strudel warm.

GLAZED APPLE JALOUSIE

A flaky glazed apple pastry, so like its counterpart that's found in Viennese confection shops.

Preheat oven to 450°; bake at 400° for 30 minutes.
Makes one 13x5-inch pastry; about 6 servings.

  ¼ cup currants or raisins
   2 teaspoons grated lemon rind
  ⅓ cup sugar
  ¼ teaspoon ground cardamom
   2 tablespoons butter or margarine
   1 package (10 ounces) frozen patty shells, thawed
   1 can (1 pound, 4 oz.) pie-sliced apples, drained
   1 egg, beaten
  ⅓ cup apple or crab apple jelly, melted

1. Preheat oven to 450°. Combine currants. lemon rind, sugar and cardamom in a small bowl. Blend in butter or margarine with a fork.
2. Overlap 3 patty shells on a lightly floured surface; overlap remaining 3 patty shells next to them so that all are overlapped. Roll out to a 13x12-inch rectangle.
3. Place a double thickness of 12-inch aluminum foil on a cooky sheet. Cut a 13x5-inch piece of pastry; place on foil. Cover center of pastry with ⅓ of the apples; sprinkle with ⅓ of the sugar mixture. Add more apples and sugar mixture; repeat for top layer.
4. From remaining pastry cut 4 strips, each 13x½ inches; cut each in half. Brush edges of pastry base with beaten egg. Place strips in 4 crisscross patterns over apples, pressing ends onto base.
5. Cut remaining pastry into 1-inch strips; place along all 4 edges of pastry base to fasten down the crisscrosses and seal in filling. Press firmly into place. Brush all surfaces with beaten egg. Carefully fold edges of foil to contain pastry. This will help keep the shape of the pastry.
6. Place in very hot oven (450°). Immediately lower heat to 400°. Bake 30 minutes, or until pastry is golden. Cool a few minutes on cooky sheet. Carefully remove from foil to wire rack. While still hot, brush entire jalousie with melted jelly.

PETALED HONEY RING

Butterflake dinner rolls can make a lovely coffee cake when you arrange them in a pan, drizzle with butter and honey, then bake until golden.

Bake at 350° for 25 minutes.
Makes one 7-cup ring.

   2 packages refrigerated butterflake dinner rolls
¼ cup raisins
   3 teaspoons grated lemon rind
   3 tablespoons honey
¼ cup (½ stick) butter or margarine, melted

1. Separate each package of rolls to make 24 even pieces. Place 12 pieces in a well-buttered 7-cup ring mold to make an even layer. Sprinkle one-third of the raisins and 1 teaspoon of the lemon rind over layer; then drizzle 1 tablespoon each of the honey and melted butter or margarine over top.
2. Make two more layers the same way; place remaining rolls on top. Drizzle remaining butter or margarine over all.
3. Bake in moderate oven (350°) 25 minutes, or until firm and golden. Loosen at once around edge with knife; invert onto a serving plate. Let stand 10 minutes. To serve, pull off layers with two forks; serve warm.

NO-BAKE "BAKED" DESSERTS

PUMPKIN PARTY TARTS

These fluffy light tarts can be made the day ahead and garnished just before serving.

Makes twelve 3-inch tarts.

   1 envelope unflavored gelatin
½ cup sugar
   1 can (1 pound) pumpkin
¾ teaspoon ground cinnamon
¼ teaspoon ground nutmeg
¼ cup orange juice
   1 pint vanilla ice cream
   2 packages (5 ounces each) pastry tart shells, (6 to a pack)

1. Combine gelatin and sugar in a medium-size saucepan. Stir in pumpkin, cinnamon, nutmeg and orange juice.
2. Cook, stirring constantly, until mixture bubbles and gelatin dissolves. Remove from heat and add ice cream, a few spoonfuls at a time.
3. Spoon pumpkin mixture into tart shells. Chill 4 hours, or overnight. Swirl whipped cream on the top of each tart, if you wish.

EASY CHEESE-FRUIT TARTS

Tiny nibbles of delicious fruit and cheese—so easy, you can put them together in no time; so good, no one will ever guess you didn't make them from scratch.

Makes six 3-inch tarts.

   2 packages (3 ounces each) cream cheese
½ cup milk
   1 container (8 ounces) raspberry or pineapple yogurt
   1 package (5 ounces) pastry tart shells (6 to a package)
     Fresh or canned fruits for garnish
   6 tablespoons apple jelly
     Chopped pistachio nuts or almonds

1. Beat cream cheese in a small bowl until soft. Gradually beat in milk; continue beating until completely smooth. Add yogurt; stir with spoon 30 seconds, or until thickened.
2. Spoon into tart shells, dividing evenly. Decorate with fruits of your choice. Melt apple jelly in a small saucepan; cool slightly, brush over fruits to glaze. Sprinkle with nuts, if you wish. Chill.

BRANDIED APRICOT TARTS

Here's another fabulous dessert you can serve when time's a problem. Cook the vanilla pudding and add a bit of brandy for a touch of elegance.

Makes six 3-inch tarts.

   1 package (3¼ ounces) vanilla pudding and pie filling
1½ cups milk
   2 tablespoons brandy
   1 can (8 ounces) apricot halves, drained
   1 package (5 ounces) pastry tart shells (6 to a package)
   2 tablespoons sugar

1. Prepare vanilla pudding and pie filling following label directions, using 1½ cups milk. Remove from heat. Add brandy.
2. Set saucepan in a pan of ice and water to speed setting. Chill, stirring often, 5 minutes, until mixture begins to mound. Or, you may press wax paper on surface of pudding, then chill in refrigerator.
3. Place 1 apricot half in bottom of each tart shell. Spoon filling into shells. Refrigerate tarts until ready to serve.
4. Just before serving, place sugar in a small skillet. Over low heat, melt sugar until it begins to caramelize. With spoon, drizzle over top of tart in a tic-tac-toe pattern.

Our tropical Islands Banana Cake is both quick and easy. Cake mix and a broiled topping cut preparation time to a minimum. Recipe in this chapter.

INDEX

A

Almond Blitz Torte, 131
Almond Cookies, 91
Almond Crescents (Danish), 35
Almond-Filled Pastry Crescents, 98
Almond Filling (Danish), 37
Almond Macaroons, 83
Almond Mazarins, 88
Almond Pound Cake, 59
Anadama Bread (Basic Recipe), 20
Anadama Cheese Bread, 20
Apple Cake, Quick, 52
Apple Jalousie, Glazed, 139
Apple Kuchen, 38
Apple-Nut Strudel, 120
Apple Pie, Devonshire, 104
Apple Pie, Sugar-Frosted, 104
Applesauce Cake, 72
Apple Streusel Muffins, 49
Apple Turnovers, Double, 115
Apricot Bow Ties (Danish), 36
Apricot-Pineapple Upside-Down Cake, 61
Apricot Pinwheels, 32-Calorie, 98
Apricot Tarts, Brandied, 140
Armenian Bread, 23
Aunt Sal's Carrot Cake, 71

B

Babas au Rhum, Petits, 128
Bacon Muffins, 49
Baking Powder Biscuits (Basic Recipe), 48
Baklava, 120
Banana Cake, Islands, 138
Banana-Nut Bread, 51
Banana-Nut Cake, 57
Biscuits, Baking Powder (Basic Recipe), 48
Black Bottom Pie, 109
Blueberry Muffins, 50
Blueberry Pie, Fresh, 107
Brandied Apricot Tarts, 140
Bridie's Irish Soda Bread, 51
Brown-eyed Susan Cookies, 91
Brownies, Our Best-Ever, 94
Brown Sugar Frosting, Fluffy, 75
Burnt Sugar Cake, 61
Burnt Sugar Frosting, 75
Busy Day Chocolate Cake, 61
Butter Cake, Golden (Basic Recipe), 57
Butterfly Cake, How to Make, 79
Buttermilk Wheat Bread, 19
Butternut Cookies, 87
Butterscotch Chews, 94

Butterscotch Cookies, 28—Calorie, 96
Butterscotch-Nut Buns, 37
Butterscotch-Walnut Cookies, 91

C

Cakes, 57-72
Cakes, How to Frost and Decorate, 76-79
Carioca Chocolate Frosting, 75
Carioca Chocolate Roll, 64
Carrot Cake, Aunt Sal's, 71
Challah Bread, 24
Cheese Bread, Anadama, 20
Cheese Danish, 36
Cheese Filling (Danish), 37
Cheese-Fruit Tarts, Easy, 140
Cheese Loaves, Little Dill, 26
Cheese Muffins, 49
Cheese-Strawberry Tart, 114
Cherry-Cheese Pie, Lattice, 114
Cherry Mocha Cake, 62
Cherry Pie, Country, 107
Cherry Pie, Deep-Dish, 107
Cherry Strudel, Quick, 139
Chess Tarts, 115
Chocolate Butter Cream Frosting, 75
Chocolate Cake, Busy Day, 61
Chocolate Chiffon Pie, 108
Chocolate Chiffon Pie, Skinny, (Low Calorie), 108
Chocolate Chip Cookies, 82
Chocolate Cream Roll, 64
Chocolate Curls, How to Make, 78
Chocolate Eclairs, 125
Chocolate Glaze, 74
Chocolate-Mint Blossoms, 95
Chocolate-Mint Jumbos, 95
Chocolate-Nut Upside-Down Cake, 62
Chocolate Torte, Double-, 132
Chocolate-Walnut Torte, 128
Chocolate-Walnut Wafers, 87
Christmas Stollen, 42
Christmas Sugar Cookies, 95
Cinnamon Prune Filling (Danish), 37
Classic Strawberry Shortcake, 48
Cloverleaf Rolls, 32
Cockscombs (Danish), 35
Coconut Cookies, 91
Coconut Cream Pie, Hawaiian, 113
Coconut Custard Pie, 110
Coconut-Jelly Cupcakes, 139
Coconut Layer Cake, 60
Coconut Macaroons, 32-Calorie, 83
Coffee-Cake Batter, Sweet (Basic Recipe), 41
Coffee Chiffon Cake, 64

Coffee Cream Filling, 73
Coffee Meringue Glacé, 133
Cookies, 82-98
Cooky Crust Pastry, 103
Cooky Cutter Patterns, and How to Make, 84-85
Cooky-Fruit Tree, cookies (see Christmas Sugar Cookies, 95)
Cooky-cutter patterns, 85; How to Make, 76
Corn Muffins, 50
Country Cherry Pie, 107
Country Corn Bread, 51
Cranberry-Pecan Bread, 52
Cream Horns Parisienne, 122
Cream Puff Pastry (Basic Recipe), 122
Cream Puffs, How to Make, 124
Crescent Rolls, 32
Crumb Buns, 38
Crumb Cake, 38
Crumb Crust, 102
Crusty French Loaves, 25
Cuban Bread, 30
Currant Batter Bread, 26

D

Danish Pastries, 34-37
Danish Pastry Dough, 34
Date-Lemon Diamonds, 94
Date-Oatmeal Cookies, 86
Date-Pecan Chews, 93
Deep-Dish Cherry Pie, 107
Deep-Dish Strawberry-Rhubarb Pie, 108
Devil's Food Cake, 63
Devonshire Apple Pie, 104
Diamond Head Fruitcake, 72
Double Apple Turnovers, 115
Double-Chocolate Torte, 132
Double-Wheat Whole Wheat Bread, 25
Drop Biscuits, 48
Dundee Cake, 72

E-F

Easy Cheese-Fruit Tarts, 140
Elephant Ears (Danish), 36
Fantan Rolls, 32
Favorite Muffins (Basic Recipe), 49
Favorite Yeast Rolls (Basic Recipe), 31
Flaky Pastry I, 102
Flaky Pastry II, 102
Florentine Cookies, 82
Fluffy Brown Sugar Frosting, 75

Fluffy 7-Minute Frosting, 75
French Loaves, Crusty, 25
Fresh Blueberry Pie, 107
Fresh Latticed Peach Pie, 103
Frostings and Fillings, 73-75
Fruit-Cheese Tarts, Easy, 140
Fruit-Filled Danish, 36

G-H

Garlic Bread, Parmesan, 29
Gingerbread, Our Best, 52
Glazed Apple Jalousie, 139
Glazed Lemon Rounds, 88
Golden Butter Cake
    (Basic Recipe), 57
Graham Cracker Crust, Slim-Down
    (Low Calorie), 103
Grandmother's White Bread, 18
Hawaiian Coconut Cream Pie, 113
High Protein Whole-Wheat
    Bread, 19
Honey Ring, Petaled, 140
Hot Cross Buns, 43
Hot-Milk Sponge Cake, 69

I-J-K

Irish Soda Bread, Bridie's, 51
Ischl Tartlets, 96
Islands Banana Cake, 138
Jelly-Coconut Cupcakes, 139
Jelly Muffins, 49
Jelly Roll (Basic Recipe), 70
Jumbo Oatmeal Crunchies, 95
King's Cake, 44
Knot Rolls, 32
Kolache Sweet Rolls, 44
Kugelhupf Coffee Cake, 41

L

Lady Baltimore Cake, 58
Lattice Cherry-Cheese Pie, 114
Lattice Pie Top, How to Make, 105
Lebkuchen Cookies, 97
Lemon Angel Pie, 134
Lemon Butter Cream Frosting, 73
Lemon Chiffon Pie (Low
    Calorie), 109
Lemon-Date Diamonds, 94
Lemon-Date Torte, 131
Lemon Filling, 74
Lemon Glaze, 74
Lemon Meringue Pie, 113
Lemon Pound Cake, 60
Lemon Roll, 70
Lemon Rose, How to Make, 78
Lemon Rounds, Glazed, 88

Lemon Tartlets Veronique, 116
Little Dill Cheese Loaves, 26
Linzer Torte, 132
Lord Baltimore Cake, 59
Lutece's Tarte à l'Orange, 121

M-N

Madeleines, 86
Marzipan Mushrooms, 76
Mayor's Braid (Danish), 37
Meadow Flowers Wedding Cake,
    126; How to Decorate, 79
Megeve Cake, 132
Mint-Chocolate Blossoms, 95
Mint-Chocolate Jumbos, 95
Mocha Cherry Cake, 62
Mocha Glaze, 74
Mocha-Nut Crown, Viennese, 122
Molasses-Spice Cookies, 83
Muffins, Favorite
    (Basic Recipe), 49
Nectarine-Raspberry Turnovers, 115
Nectarine Streusel Pie, 104
New England Pumpkin-Nut Pie, 113
Nöel Wreath Cookies, 82
Nut-Apple Strudel, 120
Nut Cake, Old-Time, 58

O

Oatmeal Crunchies, Jumbo, 95
Oatmeal-Date Cookies, 86
Old-Fashioned Sponge Cake, 63
Old-Time Nut Cake, 58
Onion Rolls, Sunday Best, 31
Orange Butter Cream Frosting,
    Rich, 73
Orange Butter Streusel Coffee
    Cake, 41
Orange Cookies, 91
Orange-Nut Cake, 60
Orange Sugar Rounds, 94
Orange Sweet Cake, 138
Our Best-Ever Brownies, 94
Our Best Gingerbread, 52

P

Panettone Fruit Bread, 43
Parmesan Garlic Bread, 29
Peaches and Cream Meringue, 133
Peach Dumplings, 116
Peach Melba Chiffon Pie, 110
Peach Pie, Fresh Latticed, 103
Peanut Butter Bars, 93
Peanut Butter Cookies, 21-
    Calorie, 86
Pecan-Cranberry Bread, 52

Pecan-Date Chews, 93
Pecan Pie, Virginia, 110
Pecan-Vanilla Wafer Crumb
    Crust, 103
Pepparkakor Cookies, 97
Petal Cake, How to Make, 79
Petaled Honey Ring, 140
Petits Babas au Rhum, 128
Pie Edgings, How to Make, 105
Pies and Tarts, 104-116
Pineapple-Apricot Upside-Down
    Cake, 61
Pineapple Cheesecake, 127
Pineapple Sponge Roll, 69
Pink Mountain Cream Frosting, 74
Plantation Fruitcake, 71
Popovers (Basic Recipe), 48
Poteca, 41
Prune Roll, Spicy, 69
Pumpkin-Nut Pie, New England, 113
Pumpkin Party Tarts, 140

Q-R

Quick Apple Cake, 52
Quick Breads, 48-52
Quick Cherry Strudel, 139
Raisin Cookies, 91
Raspberry Meringue Bars, 93
Raspberry Meringue Cake, 134
Raspberry-Nectarine Turnovers, 115
Rhubarb-Strawberry Pie,
    Deep-Dish, 108
Ribbon Spice Cake, 70
Rich Orange Butter Cream
    Frosting, 73
Royal Frosting, 75
Rum Butter Cream Frosting, 73
Rum Glaze, 74
Rye Bread, Scandinavian, 24
Rye Twist, Two-Tone, 30

S

Savarin with Strawberries and
    Cream, 126
Scandinavian Rye Bread, 24
Scones, 48
Scotch Shortbread, 98
Sesame Butter Fingers, 49
Skinny Chocolate Chiffon Pie
    (Low Calorie), 108
Slim-Down Graham Cracker Crust
    (Low Calorie), 103
Sour Cream Pastry, 103
Sour Cream-Walnut Cheesecake, 127
Sourdough Bread, 20
Sourdough Starter, 23
Spice Cake, Ribbon, 70

INDEX

Spice-Molasses Cookies, 83
Spicy Prune Roll, 69
Springerle Cookies, 96
Sponge Cake, Old-Fashioned, 63
Spritz Bonbons, 87
Spritz Slims, 87
Strawberries and Cream Cake, 58
Strawberry Butter Cream
    Frosting, 73
Strawberry Cheese Tart, 114
Strawberry Chiffon Pie, 109
Strawberry Cream Puffs, 125
Strawberry-Rhubarb Pie,
    Deep-Dish, 108
Strawberry Roll, 70
Strawberry Rosette, How To
    Make, 78
Strawberry Shortcake, Classic, 48
Sugar and Spice Cookies, 91
Sugar Buns, 38
Sugar Cookies, Christmas, 95
Sugar Cookies, Vanilla
    (Basic Recipe), 91
Sugar-Frosted Apple Pie, 104
Sugar Icing, 74
Sugar Orange Rounds, 94
Sunday Best Onion Rolls, 31
Swedish Limpa Bread, 29
Sweet Coffee-Cake Batter
    (Basic Recipe), 41
Sweet Yeast Dough
    (Basic Recipe), 37

T-U-V

Taos Bread, 23
Tarte à l'Orange, Lutece's, 121
Thimble Cookies, 88
Two-Tone Rye Twist, 30
Valentine Cake, How to Make, 79
Vanilla Butter Cream Frosting
    (Basic Recipe), 73
Vanilla Sugar Cookies
    (Basic Recipe), 91
Vanilla Wafer-Pecan Crumb Crust,
    103
Vienna Crescent Loaves, 26
Viennese Mocha-Nut Crown, 122
Virginia Pecan Pie, 110

W-X-Y-Z

Walnut-Butterscotch Cookies, 91
Walnut-Chocolate Torte, 128
Walnut-Chocolate Wafers, 87
Walnut Coffee Cake, 138
Walnut-Sour Cream Cheesecake, 127
Wedding Cake, Meadow Flowers,
    126; How to Decorate, 79
Wheat Bread, Buttermilk, 19
Wheat Germ Muffins, 50
White Bread, Grandmother's, 18
White Mountain Cream Frosting
    (Basic Recipe), 74
Whole Wheat Bread, Double-
    Wheat, 31
Whole-Wheat Bread, High
    Protein, 19
Whole Wheat Muffins, 50
Yeast Breads, Rolls and Coffee
    Cakes, 18-44
Yeast Dough, Sweet
    (Basic Recipe), 37
Yeast Rolls, Favorite
    (Basic Recipe), 31
Yorkshire Pudding, 48

ACKNOWLEDGMENTS

Pages 66-67: "Molinillo" hot
chocolate mixers, courtesy of the
Chocolate Manufacturers
Association of the United States;
"Windmills and Landscapes of
Holland", Dutch tiles courtesy of
Country Floors, Inc., 300 East 61st
Street, New York, N.Y. 10021.
Page 112: Dolly Arm Wicker Chair
and Pedestal Table courtesy of
Walters Wicker Wonderland, 991
Second Avenue, New York, N.Y.
10022.
Page 121: Tarte à l'Orange courtesy
of Lutece, New York, New York.
Page 124: "Sax Pink" china courtesy
of Ginori Fifth Avenue, 711 Fifth
Avenue, New York, N.Y. 10022.